Praise for *Master Your Motivation*

"I've performed at the Oscars several times and toured the world with artists such as Justin Timberlake. But *Master Your Motivation* emphasizes that even as a professional dancer, the real reason I practice every day isn't for those big moments alone. I was energized by remembering to reflect on my life credo: why walk, when you can dance? Now I can apply that important insight to everything I do!"
—**Ava Bernstine, professional dancer and choreographer**

"*Master Your Motivation* teaches each of us that when it comes to motivation, the quality of our motivation matters—and through the skill of motivation, we can shift our motivation anytime we choose! Our tribe flourishes when every member of the tribe thrives through optimal motivation."
—**Garry Ridge, President and CEO, WD-40 Company, and coauthor of *Helping People Win at Work***

"In Susan's last book, *Why Motivating People Doesn't Work . . . and What Does*, I keyed in on debunking the myth 'It's not personal; it's just business.' As a business owner, 'If it's business, it's personal' because my work and personal life are both guided by the same values. Now, *Master Your Motivation* gives me the practical skills and tools to guide *everything* I do. Continuously evolving through mindfulness is keeping my passion alive!"
—**Lynn Hutton, business owner and CFO, InnovaSystems International, LLC**

"*Master Your Motivation* is a wake-up call about the nature of motivation. The techniques Susan offers in this groundbreaking book work—I have personally seen people's motivation transformed, allowing them to be more productive and personally fulfilled in their endeavors. She blazes a trail that leads to a new understanding of motivation that everyone can follow, myself included."
—**Tom Hood, Deputy Director, Field Sales Leadership Development, Bayer**

"To realize that motivation is both a choice and a skill was a true gift. The feeling that I can manage my own well-being, independent of others, is true power. Thank you, Susan!"
—**Mattias Dahlgren, cofounder and CEO, Great Leaders**

"I loved Susan's last book, *Why Motivating People Doesn't Work . . . and What Does*. Our leaders use it to guide their one-to-one goal sessions—which improved our employee work passion scores dramatically. *Master Your Motivation* brings Susan's groundbreaking model to everyone, along with the skills and tools to apply to both personal and professional goals on a regular basis."

—**Chris Wollerman, CEO, Inspire Software**

"*Master Your Motivation* teaches all of us, no matter our role, that we can apply the skill of motivation to thrive. But what resonates most for me is the science behind why a strong sense of personal purpose and an investment in deeper relationships are such powerful tools for achieving our goals."

—**Cheryl Bachelder, former CEO, Popeyes Louisiana Kitchen, Inc., and author of *Dare to Serve***

"I believe this is not 'just another book on motivation' but something that is indeed unique and profoundly inspirational. Many aha moments!"

—**Karen Mathis, fashion designer and stylist, powerofappearance.com**

"I can personally attest to the power of Susan's work on motivation in my own life. I am so excited that through this book, more people will learn about the life-changing skill of motivation."

—**Nermine Zakhary, Vice President of Professional Development, Xerox Leadership Association**

MASTER YOUR *MOTIVATION*

Three Scientific Truths for Achieving Your Goals

Susan Fowler

Berrett–Koehler Publishers, Inc.

Berrett-Koehler Publishers, Inc.
1333 Broadway, Suite 1000, Oakland, CA 94612-1921
Tel: (510) 817-2277   Fax: (510) 817-2278   www.bkconnection.com

ORDERING INFORMATION
Quantity sales. Special discounts are available on quantity purchases by corporations, associations, and others. For details, contact the "Special Sales Department" at the Berrett-Koehler address above.
Individual sales. Berrett-Koehler publications are available through most bookstores. They can also be ordered directly from Berrett-Koehler: Tel: (800) 929-2929; Fax: (802) 864-7626; www.bkconnection.com.
Orders for college textbook / course adoption use. Please contact Berrett-Koehler: Tel: (800) 929-2929; Fax: (802) 864-7626.

Distributed to the U.S. trade and internationally by Penguin Random House Publisher Services.

Berrett-Koehler and the BK logo are registered trademarks of Berrett-Koehler Publishers, Inc.

Berrett-Koehler books are printed on long-lasting acid-free paper. When it is available, we choose paper that has been manufactured by environmentally responsible processes. These may include using trees grown in sustainable forests, incorporating recycled paper, minimizing chlorine in bleaching, or recycling the energy produced at the paper mill.

Library of Congress Cataloging-in-Publication Data
Names: Fowler, Susan, 1951– author.
Title: Master your motivation : three scientific truths for achieving your goals / Susan Fowler.
Description: First Edition. | Oakland, CA : Berrett-Koehler Publishers, 2019.
Identifiers: LCCN 2018058495 | ISBN 9781523098620 (paperback)
Subjects: LCSH: Motivation (Psychology) | BISAC: BUSINESS & ECONOMICS / Motivational. | SELF-HELP / Motivational & Inspirational. | PSYCHOLOGY / Applied Psychology.
Classification: LCC BF503 .F689 2019 | DDC 153.1/534—dc23
LC record available at https://lccn.loc.gov/2018058495

FIRST EDITION

25 24 23 22 21 20 19   10 9 8 7 6 5 4 3 2 1

Text designer & typesetting: Girl of the West Productions
Editor: PeopleSpeak
Cover designer: Emma Smith

CONTENTS

Foreword by Jean-Paul Richard
with Jacques Forest. v

Introduction—Why Motivation Science Matters. 1

Part One—The Truth about Motivation 5
  1 Three Scientific Truths 7
  2 Motivation Isn't What You Think 17
  3 Create Choice 24
  4 Create Connection 30
  5 Create Competence. 37

Part Two—Motivation Is a Skill 43
  6 Identify Your Outlook. 47
  7 Shift Your Outlook 68
  8 Reflect on Your Outlook 88

Part Three—What's Stopping You? 109
  9 I Can't Shift. 113
  10 Beware Fatal Distractions 126
  11 Work Hazards 139
  12 Can People Change? 150

Afterword by Ken Blanchard. 159

Notes. 163
Resources. 169
Acknowledgments. 170
Index. 173
About the Author 177

*To my siblings, Dee Dee, Terri, and Kip,
whose acceptance of my quirky need to share
whatever I was learning helped me discover my
inherent motivation for teaching. And to my
beloved Drea, who continues to patiently
partner with me on this life journey.*

FOREWORD
Jean-Paul Richard with Jacques Forest

My experience as head coach of the Swedish Olympic team for the Vancouver 2010 Olympics was totally different than coaching the Canadian team in Sochi four years later. The difference wasn't the caliber of athletes competing or the flag I coached under, although being a Canadian coach for a foreign country competing in Canada added extra scrutiny! Both Olympics required a meticulous and rigorous approach to the technical and physical preparation of my program and athletes. In both cases, our goals were high, and the athletes were world class. But the two experiences were as different as night and day—and so were the results. The big difference between my two Olympic experiences was helping my team and athletes master their motivation and, perhaps even more important, learning to master my own motivation so I could be an effective coach. I think my story perfectly illustrates what you can gain from Susan's work and this book.

In Vancouver 2010, our high-caliber athletes had the opportunity to achieve great performances in the name of Sweden. One of the main goals and motivation in our mind (consciously or unconsciously) was to win medals. The pressure to win, not disappoint people—indeed, an entire team, sport, country!—who were supporting us was increased by my need to attain the status of being an Olympic medalist coach and gain the recognition of my peers, not to mention funding and a contract renewal. As you will learn from reading this book, I was partly blinded because my eyes were constantly on the tangible reward of winning medals and the intangible rewards of status and image. The athletes I coached also didn't receive 100 percent of what I could give them. Under the pressure, I adopted behaviors that limited communication with my athletes—and kept me in only partial touch with my own feelings and emotions.

Using Susan's term, my "suboptimal motivation," fueled by the constant state pressure of the traditional sports system and typical Olympic environment, infected the motivation of everyone around me, creating a chain of events, a loss of energy and concentration, and ultimately limited expression of the athletes' full promise. Focusing on winning medals led to not winning any. Regretfully, we failed to achieve our potential.

I knew I had to find a way to escape the pressure and the negative emotions it generates. The solution came at the beginning of the Olympic cycle on the road to Sochi 2014. I was back in Canada to lead the women's freestyle ski team when I discovered the new science of motivation. With the help of Dr. Jacques Forest, a leading researcher in the field and a professor of motivational psychology in Montreal, I came to understand the role motivation had played in Vancouver. In preparation for Sochi, Dr. Forest and I developed a program to help my staff and athletes shift their focus from winning medals to satisfying their psychological needs for autonomy, relatedness, and competence, or what Susan refers to as Choice, Connection, and Competence.

With our focus on what really matters, on February 8, 2014, in Sochi, Russia, we won two Olympic medals (gold and silver) and exceeded all expectations. We learned that winning is a by-product of mastering your motivation—not the reason for your motivation.

I share my story because Dr. Forest and I discovered Susan's first book on motivation, *Why Motivating People Doesn't Work*

. . . *and What Does*, when it was published in late 2014. We were thrilled. For the first time, someone had unraveled and captured the complex science of motivation for leaders—and more importantly, provided a framework and process for applying it with others. Susan's book went on to become a bestseller translated into fourteen languages, which is testimony to its quality of being far-reaching and easy to understand. I continued to use it with the Canadian Olympic team, and Dr. Forest uses it in his teaching and consulting. Today, the book is still on my desk and helps me in my work as the head of the training programs for Cirque du Soleil.

Now Susan has evolved her ideas and approach to applying motivation science to benefit every individual. I am convinced this book will help you achieve your goals for the right reasons. If you are an athlete, it will help you enjoy the process of training and competing by using your full potential. If you have kids, it will help you give them the gift of optimal motivation. No matter your role, it will give you access to principles for creating a workplace where you can thrive. Ultimately, Susan's approach to motivation, based on real science, will help you be an optimally functioning human being. Now that athletes and coaches have a resource to help them master their motivation, I look forward to hearing them tell their own success stories.

Jean-Paul Richard, head of artist training programs, Cirque du Soleil, cofounder of reROOT Inc., and Olympic medalist coach (Freestyle skiing, Moguls, Sochi 2014)

Jacques Forest, PhD, professor-researcher and motivational psychologist, ESG UQAM, and partner at reROOT Inc.

Why Motivation Science Matters

Motivation is at the heart of everything you do and want to do but don't. Motivation is also the reason you do things you wish you didn't.

Millions of books, podcasts, seminars, workshops, incentives, contests, rewards, coaching sessions, diet plans, and self-help groups attest to our desire to master our motivation. They also reflect our lack of understanding about what motivation is and how to use it for achieving our goals.

What's missing in most approaches to motivation is a unifying theory and foundational model explaining why a technique works or doesn't. How else will you know when advice is valid, reliable, or worthy of pursuit? We need motivation science—ideas and techniques we can rely on because they are backed by empirical evidence and demonstrated over time to work across a variety of cultures, situations, personalities, genders, and generations.

Of course, a plethora of motivation theories have been touted over the years. Unfortunately, some of the most commonly accepted theories are outdated or have been proven inadequate or downright wrong. For example, we're only now realizing the drawbacks and hidden costs of relying on extrinsic motivation in the workplace. External forms of motivation, often referred to as "carrots" (rewards, incentives, power, status, and image) and "sticks" (pressure, guilt, fear, and threats) were popularized back in the 1940s by B. F. Skinner, who used training animals as a model for motivating human beings. Now we know that extrinsic motivators do not promote real or permanent change and are more likely to diminish the quality of your results, performance, creativity, innovation, and well-being—even in the short term. And, despite Abraham Maslow's contributions to motivation science, his hierarchy of needs, the most popular motivation model in the world, has never been empirically proven.[1]

Enter Dr. Edward Deci and Dr. Richard Ryan and thousands of self-determination theory (SDT) researchers who have rigorously pursued understanding the nature of our motivation and explaining how it really works.[2] Their discoveries using a variety of scientific methods, including qualitative and quantitative academic research, neuroscience, and psychological clinical practice, represent the most comprehensive breakthroughs in motivation science. The three scientific truths revealed in this book are at the core of their groundbreaking research. You will come to understand these truths in the coming pages, but that won't be enough to master your motivation.

As the old saying goes, to know and not to do is not to know. Good science is applied science. Understanding the three scientific truths is only the beginning. You also need to know how to apply the truths—what to do differently than you've done in the past. But even well-intentioned approaches to good applied science face the challenge of unraveling complex ideas and translating them into digestible nuggets. Oversimplifying great science to the point it loses its potency poses a challenge. For example, you might have heard about two types of motivation, intrinsic and extrinsic:

■ Intrinsic motivation, considered the preferred type of motivation, occurs when you do something for the pure enjoyment of doing it, without the need for or promise of an external reward.

■ Extrinsic motivation, considered the less preferred type of motivation, occurs when you need an external prompt or reason for doing something you don't naturally enjoy doing.

However, boiling motivation down to its nubs renders it almost impossible to use. For example, I'm sure you can identify a goal or task that will never be intrinsically motivating to you: dragging yourself out of bed in the morning to attend a staff meeting you think is a waste of time, being forced to leave your family on a Sunday for a business trip, completing bureaucratic paperwork that steals time from your "real" job, or giving up french fries and comfort food to lose weight for your upcoming school reunion.

Simplifying motivation into two types, intrinsic and extrinsic, presents a conundrum when you aren't intrinsically motivated. Your only fallback position is extrinsic motivation. And if extrinsic motivation is your only other option, you are more likely to succumb to traditional and outdated techniques to compensate for your lack of intrinsic motivation—perpetuating those proverbial extrinsic carrots and sticks to motivate yourself and others.

The challenge this book takes on is to simplify motivation science without oversimplifying it. Yes, this new and cutting-edge science is more complex—and reaching the other side of complexity takes time, experimentation, and diligence. That's why I've spent decades working with some of the best minds in the world to develop a unique framework and approach to motivation that has proven both empirically sound and practical to use.

When my book *Why Motivating People Doesn't Work . . . and What Does* was published in 2014, its focus was to teach leaders how to nurture a work environment where people are more likely to experience optimal motivation, produce results, and thrive.

The focus of this book is you. Instead of waiting for someone else to shape your motivation, you will learn the skills for mastering your own motivation. The ideas have been vetted by individuals from across the globe in almost every type of industry you can imagine, representing people of all ages and generations. Many of them share their firsthand accounts in this book. My greatest hope is that you will discover and embrace the insights and tools to master your motivation, improve the quality of your life, and, in the process, find joy in contributing to a world that works for all.

The Truth about Motivation

What if you were offered three elixirs promising to transform your everyday experiences? Imagine you suddenly understood the real reason dieting doesn't work and what does. Imagine you grasped why you tear your hair out each month to submit expense reports on time and how to meet those deadlines while not losing your hair. Imagine discovering peace of mind.

What if you were told these magic potions could help you generate the positive energy you need to achieve your goals, promote your mental and physical health, experience well-being, be more creative, improve your work performance, and fuel work passion? The only caveat is that the three elixirs must be used in unison—each potion by itself is beneficial, but real magic happens when you combine them. Would you be intrigued enough to explore the possibilities?

The three scientific truths at the heart of mastering your motivation are like the three elixirs. Using them in combination could transform the way you approach goals and live your life. These three scientific truths are not a magic cure-all that is too good to be true; they are backed up by empirical research and testimonials from people with firsthand experience. Frankly, the three scientific truths to master your motivation are even better than elixirs because they work like magic but are real, don't cost a fortune, and won't cause harmful side effects. Their discovery represents one of the greatest breakthroughs in motivation science.

1.

Three Scientific Truths

Are you lazy? Do you think most people are basically lazy? Do you enjoy being disengaged at work? Do you think millions of people worldwide enjoy being disengaged? Is that why we need to be prodded, bribed, praised, and pushed into doing what we're tasked to do? If managers did not hold us accountable for achieving our goals, do you think we would slack off? If you answer any of these questions yes, maybe your basic beliefs about human motivation need updating.

You have a natural yearning to thrive—thriving is your human nature. Being bored or disengaged isn't thriving. Being lazy isn't thriving. Resenting hard work isn't thriving. The truth is, no one wants to be bored, disengaged, or lazy. At our core, we don't resent hard work. We welcome productive and meaningful work, even when it's hard. We appreciate meaningful challenges. We even want to be accountable—we just don't like being *held* accountable! We want to contribute, feel fulfilled, and grow and learn every day. We long to thrive.

Recognizing our nature to thrive leads to a critical question: How do I thrive? Now, thanks to groundbreaking research, we know the answer. And, it's different than what we've been led to believe. Thriving doesn't depend on money, power, or status. Thriving doesn't come from promotions, perks, or driving for results. Thriving certainly doesn't happen through pressure, tension, or fear—or even willpower or discipline. Thriving requires Choice, Connection, and Competence.

Motivation is the energy to act. Choice, connection, and competence generate the high-quality motivation (energy) you need to thrive. Your high-quality motivation—and the energy to achieve your goals and find meaning in their pursuit—depends on creating choice, connection, and competence.

> **To master your motivation, create choice, connection, and competence.**

Our need for choice, connection, and competence has been verified scientifically, and I think you'll resonate personally with the definition and description of each scientific truth.

1. *First scientific truth: you need to create choice.* You have an innate need to perceive you have choices, recognize and feel you have options within boundaries, and have a sense of control over what is happening at any time: "I am the source of my behavior." When you don't create choice, your energy is diminished, and you are less likely to achieve your goals.

2. *Second scientific truth: you need to create connection.* You have an innate need to feel a sense of belonging and genuine connection to others without concerns about ulterior motives, pursue goals aligned to meaningful values and a noble purpose, and contribute to something greater than yourself. When you don't create connection, your energy is compromised, and even if you

achieve your goals, you are less likely to find the experience meaningful or worth repeating.

3. *Third scientific truth: you need to create competence.* You have an innate need to feel effective at managing everyday situations, demonstrate skill over time, and feel a sense of growth and learning every day. When you don't create competence, your energy is blocked, and your frustration at not being able to meet challenges or make progress puts achieving long-term goals at risk.

The evidence supporting the three scientific truths at the center of your motivation is compelling, but all you need to do is look around you. Notice that when you create choice, connection, and competence, you feel a sense of well-being, are in a flow state, or experience deep-seated peace. On the flip side, observe that when one or more of the three truths are diminished, you feel pressure, tension, stress, loneliness, pride, superiority, despair, fear, anger, or frustration.

When you create choice, connection, and competence, you flourish. When they are eroded, you languish.

The Three Truths—Everywhere You Look

Have you ever bought a new car and then noticed every car on the road that looks like yours? This phenomenon is called reticular activation—a function of your brain that filters information. Your reticular activating system is at work when you are in a noisy room, someone mentions your name, and you snap to attention. You can use reticular activation to confirm the power of creating choice, connection, and competence.

Through reticular activation, you will probably see children through new eyes. A baby grabbing a spoon to feed himself—even when he can't find his mouth—is creating choice. A two-year-old who's talking to you when you're not looking at her creates connection by grabbing your face and turning it so she can see your eyes. A toddler learning to walk creates competence when he gets up after he falls, without crying—expressing his joy of learning something new and exciting.

You can also recognize how creating choice, connection, and competence plays a role when you are moved emotionally by a movie, book, or news story. In 2011, I teared up while watching a CNN interview of fourteen-year-old Malala Yousafzai. She had gained fame in Pakistan by speaking out for her rights. She claimed her right to play, sing, and go to the market. But her voice was loudest for her right to education, which was forbidden to females by the Taliban. She explained how her people needed her and how, by speaking out, she could make a difference, especially to young girls who she felt had the right to learn. My reticular activating system went on high alert: Malala was clearly articulating her need to create choice (to choose her own path), connection (to make a difference in the world), and competence (to learn, grow, and be educated).

A year later, Malala was shot in the head by a terrorist to silence her voice. But she didn't die. Her story, *I Am Malala: The Girl Who Stood Up for Education and Was Shot by the Taliban*, is an eloquent expression of our need for choice, connection, and competence. In 2014, she became the youngest person to ever win the Nobel Peace Prize. As an international advocate for children standing up for their rights, finding meaning in their lives, and making education a priority, Malala continues to inspire millions to create choice, connection, and competence.

The Three Truths—Gone Missing

Has someone ever tripped your trigger, pushing all the right buttons, and you didn't handle it well? Unfortunately, my story—how I failed to self-regulate and eroded any chance of creating choice, connection, and competence—may sound too familiar.

A director of sales, whom we will call Stacy because that's her real name, asked me to consult as a subject-matter expert (SME) with a potential new client. We'll call the potential client Diane, which isn't her real name. Stacy scheduled a one-hour call for 2:00 p.m. the following Wednesday. I prepared diligently, as I don't take being an SME lightly. I studied the notes Stacy sent me. I reviewed information about the organization from a variety of sources, including its website and latest annual report. I took the time to generate thoughtful ideas to discuss.

Stacy and I were on the call early to be sure we were prepared. At 2:10 p.m., Stacy pinged Diane to see if there was a problem or misunderstanding about the time. We were about to give up when a beep-beep announced Diane was finally joining the call. Stacy graciously greeted Diane: "Diane, I am so glad you could make the call today. As you know, I invited Susan Fowler, our subject-matter expert on motivation and engagement, to discuss ideas with you. She's read the notes from our previous meeting and done her homework, but first, let me introduce you and clarify your expectations for today."

Before Stacy could complete her introduction, Diane interrupted: "Stacy, I don't have time for this. I have a hard stop at 2:30. Besides, I have changed my mind. I've decided to go in a different direction."

I was stunned—not just at Diane's sudden change in direction but at her rude behavior. I didn't know what to say in that moment, but it didn't matter because Diane launched into what she was thinking and what she wanted to do. None of it made any sense to me. I had questions and concerns, but I couldn't get a word in edgewise, and we were coming up on her 2:30 p.m. hard stop. That's when I noticed a *physiological disturbance*. I use this term to describe my body's reaction to a highly emotional experience. The disturbance started in my gut. As I got more frustrated with Diane, I could feel the negative energy rise into my chest. My frustration grew into anger, and as the roiling energy reached my face, I could feel it flush.

Suddenly, I heard myself boldly (and loudly) interrupting: "Stacy, Diane, excuse me. It seems Diane knows exactly what she wants; there's nothing I can do to help her, so I'll let you two finish the call." Then I hung up.

Again I was stunned. I had just hung up on a potential new client and abandoned Stacy. Yes, Diane was aggravating, but I had never done anything like this before. I was beside myself. I paced around my home office to let off steam. I was infuri-ated—at Diane and myself. Before I knew it, I found myself in my kitchen with the refrigerator door open, declaring *"I am so hungry!"*

The blast of cold air from the fridge induced a moment of mindfulness. I realized nothing in that refrigerator could pos-sibly satisfy my hunger. Everything I'd learned about moti-vation came to light. I suddenly understood what happened during that short phone call. My choice, connection, and competence had been eroded:

- I didn't perceive that I had any options—in fact, just the opposite. I felt Diane unfairly controlled the situation, which eroded my sense of choice.

- Diane and I obviously did not align in any meaningful way—in fact, just the opposite. She made no attempt to collaborate or show appreciation for my efforts, which undermined my sense of connection.

▪ After all my efforts, I didn't have the opportunity to demonstrate my subject-matter expertise or discuss my great ideas—in fact, just the opposite. I felt inadequate and dealt with the situation by hanging up, which destroyed my sense of competence.

Staring into my fridge, I came face-to-face with the truth: I needed to master my motivation. I realized how my motivation had fluctuated during my Diane debacle because my sense of choice, connection, and competence had fluctuated.

When Stacy first asked for my help, I freely and consciously made the decision to engage with her and her client (I created choice). I was energized by the value of being of service and felt grateful that Stacy had reached out to me for help (I created connection). I was eager for the opportunity to teach the client what I knew about her organization's issues, explain how our approach could make a difference, and learn something new about her situation in the process (I created competence). By creating choice, connection, and competence, I felt optimal motivation.

Within minutes after Diane joined the call, I lost control of my emotions, felt powerless, and in the end failed to self-regulate (choice was eroded). My image and ego were crushed, I felt isolated and ashamed, and I realized I'd done more harm than good (connection was eroded). I was devastated that I had failed to practice what I teach—I questioned the validity of my knowledge and skill, wondering if I was a fraud (competence was eroded). By not creating choice, connection, and competence, I felt suboptimal motivation.

I hadn't yet learned to master my motivation. But recognizing what happened was a major learning moment.

Acknowledging my alternatives, I wrote a confessional email to Stacy—creating choice. I asked for forgiveness and offered to serve behind the scenes in any way I could—creating connection. Stacy took me up on my offer, and I coached one of my colleagues as she took on the account—creating competence. (Stacy gave me permission to share this story and has become an advocate for teaching others how to create choice, connection, and competence.)

> **Create choice, connection, and competence**
> **to master your motivation and thrive.**
> **Their absence is literally bad for your health.**

You might be wondering, If the three truths of choice, connection, and competence are the magic elixirs for mastering your motivation, why isn't everyone taking advantage of them? The answer lies in how deeply embedded outdated ideas about motivation are in our beliefs and traditional approaches to motivation. The time has come to challenge what we think motivation is and isn't.

SCIENCE SAYS

Self-determination theory is an encompassing and overarching theory of human motivation that has been tested and refined for the last forty-five years. This way of seeing human beings as having a natural tendency toward growth, thriving, and self-actualization can be applied in domains as varied as health, education, psychotherapy, counseling, video games, parenting, physical activity, and sports, as well as work, where most adults spend the biggest part of their lives.

This theory, tested in dozens of countries in all spheres of life, tells us that we can have high-quality reasons (joy and meaning) but lower-quality reasons (ego and rewards) to do what we do. We reap benefits (optimal functioning and happiness) by promoting the high-quality reasons but will not promote these positive consequences, and even promote negative consequences (suboptimal functioning and sadness), by inviting the low-quality reasons.

Global studies of these high-quality and low-quality motivations show that no matter your culture, age, gender, job, or organization, joy and meaning are better than ego and rewards.

Your brain needs "psychological vitamins" to increase the high-quality motivations. These nutrients are the universal basic psychological needs of autonomy (being self-directed and authentic, which I refer to as choice), relatedness (having a sense of belonging and meaning, which I refer to as connection), and competence (feeling and being efficient at what we do, which I also refer to as competence). These needs are important for everyone, everywhere, all the time, just as a plant needs sun, soil, and water to grow. When you have sufficient psychological vitamins (i.e., your psychological needs are satisfied), you increase the likelihood of experiencing joy and high performance. Moreover, when you do not have psychological vitamins and rely on psychological junk food (i.e., your psychological needs are frustrated), ego and rewards are more likely to be the main drivers of your action, leading you to experience more negative experiences.[1]

——————————————■——————————————

Discover more about the three scientific truths by visiting the *Master Your Motivation* page at www.susanfowler.com.

2.

Motivation Isn't What You Think

Last week, you disciplined yourself to work out three times. You willed yourself to complete a budget over the weekend. You were excited to enter a sales contest. After admiring your abs, submitting the budget, and winning the sales trip, you credited your success to willpower, discipline, and your competitive nature.

Fast forward to the following month. You find yourself summoning more willpower to rework the budget after your manager rejected it, conjuring more discipline to get to the gym after work, and scavenging for more incentives to pump you up for making another sales call. After driving yourself to achieve your goals, you realize that maybe motivation isn't what you think.

At the risk of challenging cherished habits, I'm asking you to explore some of your basic beliefs about motivation and alternatives to discipline, willpower, and external rewards such as making more money, winning a prize, or gaining power. You can use these traditional methods to motivate yourself, but you risk undermining your choice, connection, and competence. To better understand what I mean, consider the nature of motivation.

Motivation is the energy to act. The quality of your energy determines the quality of your motivation.

Eating a candy bar produces energy—but eating a handful of almonds generates longer-lasting and more efficient energy. For example, when your physical stamina dips, if you grab a candy bar, soft drink, or french fries, your blood sugar shoots up and so does your energy. Then what happens? You crash. Your blood sugar drops below what it was before, so you need more sugar, caffeine, or carbs. A similar phenomenon occurs with motivation—how you fuel your psychic energy produces either a junk food motivational rush or a healthier alternative.

> **When it comes to motivation, the quality of your energy is what matters.**

Mastering your motivation requires letting go of the outdated notion that motivation depends on *how much* motivation you have. When you say, "I'm not motivated to exercise," you assume you don't have enough energy, so you need something to give you more energy. But motivation science says we have that all wrong. A seismic revolution in our understanding of motivation occurs when we know that what matters most is not the quantity but the quality of the energy that fuels our motivation. When it comes to motivation, quality matters.

Time Out for a New Language of Motivation

Before taking these ideas further, I have a proposal for you. Have you ever listened to people talk who work in an industry different than yours? They seem to speak an alien language—acronyms and jargon that can leave you feeling left out of the conversation. A big challenge in writing this book is finding words that describe a different approach to motivation that doesn't leave you scratching your head—or worse, putting the book down.

We need words that reflect the advances made in motivation science and a new paradigm for understanding motivation. We need language that liberates us from outdated terminology originally established by studying animals in the 1940s (*carrots* and *sticks*) and from oversimplified terms that can't be practically applied (*intrinsic* and *extrinsic* motivation). So I ask you to accept updated words and phrases that relate a fresh perspective and modern framework of motivation, including the terms in figure 1.

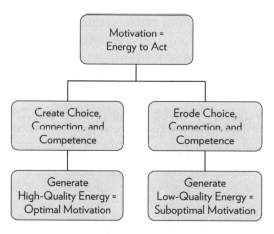

Figure 1   **New language of motivation**

As the figure shows, creating choice, connection, and competence generates *high-quality energy*, which leads to *optimal motivation*.

Optimal motivation delivers productivity and results but also increased creativity and innovation, an enhanced sense of well-being, and higher levels of work passion that sustain your high performance and help you thrive.

On the other hand, eroding choice, connection, and competence leads to suboptimal motivation. Traditional ways of motivating ourselves—from relying on external motivators such as winning rewards, acquiring power, or achieving status to succumbing to negative forces such as pressure, fear, or shame—tend to result in suboptimal motivation. Appreciating the difference between optimal motivation and suboptimal motivation has real-world implications.

SCIENCE SAYS

Frequent optimally motivating experiences increase well-being more than stable conditions such as a high salary or prestigious title. The more often you experience optimal motivation—in moment-to-moment interactions with coworkers, ongoing projects, or daily contributions—the more likely you are to experience well-being and achieve measurable results.[1] Individuals who experience optimal motivation and well-being at work, when compared to their coworkers who do not, deliver higher productivity and creativity.[2] They tend to be more satisfied and engaged in their jobs.[3]

Simply put, you are less likely to attain your desired results with suboptimal motivation, which takes a toll on you emotionally and physically—in both the short and long term. You are more likely to achieve your goals with optimal motivation—and to experience positive well-being in the process.[4]

Optimal motivation is the healthy alternative to suboptimal motivation. Unfortunately, you could be undermining your energy with a steady diet of junk food motivation and not even realize it.

Could You Be Bingeing on Junk Food Motivation?

As a regional manager for a large manufacturing company, Nick had steadily made his way up the leadership ladder. But over the years, all his performance reviews cited the same area for development—budgeting. Nick simply hates what he perceives as bureaucratic paperwork, especially budgets that seem outdated as soon as they are submitted.

Intellectually, Nick understands that budgets are important to the company and a requirement of his role. Still, he procrastinates and finds himself under pressure to give up a weekend crunching numbers—and resenting every minute of it.

Reflecting on his motivation, Nick realized he was avoiding the issue until the deadline approached. Then the pressure kicked in, mixed with a flood of emotions, including fear of not delivering on his manager's expectations, shame over demanding that his team turn in reports on time when he didn't make his own deadlines, regret that he wasn't a better role model, and disappointment in himself for not acting on his good intentions.

Nick had been bingeing on a junk food motivation concoction of discipline and willpower fueled by negative emotions of fear, frustration, anger, resentment, and regret. This was not only not the best way to spend a weekend but also a lousy way to generate high-quality energy and optimal motivation. As Nick discovered, his issue was the quality of his motivation.

Nick had resorted to willpower and discipline, believing they were his only alternatives to force himself to do something he didn't naturally enjoy doing. Nick needed to power through the budget because he felt he had to (no choice). He found little to no personal meaning in the process (no connection). He was overwhelmed by the process and felt inadequate (no competence). When the reason for your motivation depends on improving your image or status, winning rewards, fear, or pressure, you erode choice, connection, and competence and generate low-quality energy. Your suboptimal motivation limits your ability to achieve your goals.

As admirable as willpower and discipline may seem, they are red flags warning you of suboptimal motivation— and reminding you that you have better alternatives.

According to research, Nick was less likely to achieve his goal with suboptimal motivation. But even if he did, the quality of his work and his mental and physical health would be compromised—and he would still dread the next budget period.

Nick realized that motivation wasn't what he thought it was. He explored reasons to complete his budgets that created choice, connection, and competence. For example, Nick's shift from suboptimal to optimal motivation was boosted when he created connection by recognizing how submitting budgets on time aligned with one of his deeply held values of being a positive role model for the people he leads.

To master your motivation, create choice, connection, and competence, which leads to the optimal motivation you need for achieving your goals.

When the reason for your motivation is based on developed values, a noble purpose, or inherent joy, you are more likely to create choice, connection, and competence and generate high-quality energy. Your optimal motivation promotes your ability to achieve your goals—and repeat them.

Learn more about the new language of motivation by visiting the *Master Your Motivation* page at www.susanfowler.com.

3

Create Choice

To master your motivation, create choice. To create choice, you need to

- Perceive you have choices
- Recognize and feel you have options within boundaries
- Feel that you are in control of your actions

Have you ever failed at a diet? You had such good intentions. What happened? The nature of most diets is to limit and dictate your choices—or that's how you may interpret your diet as you monitor each mouthful. As soon as you declare, "I can't have that; I'm on a diet," you have eroded choice. If you think you can't have a muffin, what's the thing you want most? You may think it's that forbidden muffin. But it's not about the muffin. It's about choice. You're hungry for choice. So you *choose* to eat the muffin. You could have chosen not to eat the muffin, but the diet told you not to eat it, so it didn't feel like real choice.

I often run late for appointments because I try to check off too many to-do items before leaving my office. Depending on your personality type and driving habits, this scene might feel familiar. The more rushed I am, the more I seem to find myself caught behind an intolerably slow driver (who's

> You have an innate need for choice—to perceive that
> you are the one controlling your actions and
> the ongoing source of your behavior,
> even when influenced by outside forces.

probably going the speed limit). I become a slow-car magnet. Next thing I notice, I am clenching the wheel of my car and mumbling something rude under my breath. What's happening? My need for speed is being impeded; choice is eroded. Start to notice how many times during a regular day you feel pressure or frustration because you lack real or perceived choice.

Choice Is Different Than Freedom

Blaming others for restricting our choices is easy to do—and sometimes it's warranted. Contesting forces that threaten freedom may be necessary. Courageous people such as Malala, Nelson Mandela, Gandhi, Martin Luther King, women speaking up in the #MeToo movement, and freedom fighters around the world throughout history have proven that there is an appropriate response to those who would rob others of basic freedom or equal rights.

But when it comes to motivation, choice is different than freedom. One of my top five favorite books of all time is *Man's Search for Meaning* by Viktor Frankl. Frankl's description of living through a World War II concentration camp changed my perspective on life. Frankl realized that even though he had no freedom as we would define freedom, his captors could not take away his choice. He chose to see the beauty of a sunrise, accept the punishment promised as he came to the aid of a fellow prisoner, and share a piece of his bread with another starving prisoner. They couldn't rob him of his autonomy—his perception of freedom. He understood that you might not be able to control your situation, but you can choose your thoughts, reactions, and perspective.[1]

> **Even if you don't have freedom,**
> **you can still experience choice.**

This may seem to be a radical idea, but the reality is that you don't have to go to work. You could choose to live off the largesse of others or to be homeless. You could decide not to support your family. You don't have to work as hard as you do. You could choose to live a less lavish and more afford-able lifestyle. Yet many of us drag ourselves out of bed in the morning with the thought "I have to go to work." No, you are exercising your choice to work, be financially independent, support your family, or live a desired lifestyle.

You don't have to pay taxes. You could choose to pay fines or risk the consequences of avoiding taxes. Yet we often complain, "I have to pay taxes." No, you are exercising your choice to live by the laws of your country and be a responsi-ble citizen.

Are You Undermining Choice?

As Viktor Frankl demonstrated, we may need to deal with demons in the world, but we also need to deal with the demons in our own mind. I find it fascinating that Frankl recommended that the Statue of Liberty on the East Coast be supplemented by the Statue of Responsibility on the West Coast.[2] Choosing how we respond to what life offers is our responsibility.

In a world crying out for effective leadership, you need to begin with the most obvious source—yourself. To avoid undermining choice, practice actions from the list below:

- Stop blaming others for my situation, feeling sorry for myself, or playing the victim.

- Learn how to deal effectively with my micromanaging manager.

- Find alternatives to external motivators such as incentives, awards, prizes, and rankings that I don't control.

- Change the reason I play the game (or pursue my goal). Don't play to win for the sake of winning. I am not in control if playing is all about gaining power, status, or image—I can't make people give me power, status, or respect. But I can create choice when I play for meaningful reasons such as the value of working hard or achieving excellence. Then, whether I win or lose the "game," I am a winner.

- Don't yield to pressure imposed from external forces— stay true to the purpose behind my goal and the values guiding how I pursue it.

- Be proactive: clarify unclear goals, ask for feedback, be a problem solver, and negotiate for authority when it's deserved.

- Don't depend on the approval of others whose opinions I don't control.

- Don't try to control people (because I can't).

- Have a promotable mindset, with an occasional preventative mindset. Unless the risks are high and time lines are short, say yes before I say no.

Good on you if you choose to not undermine choice and not feel powerless, used, victimized, pressured, threatened, or limited. But to guarantee you create choice, you can also deal with it directly.

Questions to Create Choice

Ask yourself targeted questions to create choice:

When it comes to my goal or situation,
1. What choices have I made?
   - If I made choices I'm glad about, why am I glad?
   - If I made choices I wish I hadn't made, why do I wish I hadn't made them?

2. What different choices could I make going forward?
   - How do I feel about those choices?
   - If I perceive I don't have any choices, why is that? Is it true or is it just my perception that it's true?

3. Do I feel the goal or situation was imposed on me?
   - If I feel imposed on by the goal or situation, where is the pressure (or fear, guilt, shame) coming from? Why do I think that is?
   - Could my behavior and actions positively impact the outcome?
   - If I feel restricted, powerless, or controlled by current boundaries, how could I gain a sense of control over the situation? Why is that important?

> **Sometimes being aware that you didn't think you had any choices is enough for you to realize you do.**

These questions create choice. Answering them is the antidote to motivation based on fear or pressure from outside forces—such as incentives, rewards, approval from others—or your own expectations. When you allow fear and pressure to drive your motivation, you are not in control and your sense of autonomy is limited. When you acknowledge that you have alternatives to drivers of suboptimal motivation, you regain your power of choice.

Visit the *Master Your Motivation* page at www.susanfowler.com to learn more about creating choice.

4.

Create Connection

To master your motivation, create connection. To create connection, you need to

- Feel a sense of belonging and genuine connection to others without concerns about ulterior motives
- Align goals and actions to meaningful values and a noble purpose
- Contribute to something greater than yourself

During dinner with a successful middle-aged man, I was surprised when he pulled out his phone, took a photo of his meal, and posted it on Instagram. He didn't seem like the social media type to me. Thirty minutes later, I understood what attracted him to Instagram. He was checking how many likes he'd received. To him, social media wasn't about connection; it was about competition, rankings, and image. His whole mood changed when he realized someone else's post had garnered more comments than his. Social media is a testament to our need for connection. But being connected isn't the same as experiencing connection.

Because we are social animals, connection is our deepest and most profound need, yet it's probably the least fulfilled in today's modern world. Connection means authentically caring about others and feeling cared for by them. Social media has the potential to promote that, but as we are apt to do, we externalize our motivation. Instead of cherishing our shared values or interests, we find that our motivation becomes dependent on external factors—on the quantity of our friends, connections, or likes, rather than the quality of our relationships. Never have we been more connected yet experienced less connection.

> **You have an innate need for connection—to care about and feel cared about by others, find meaning in everyday moments, and experience a sense of unity as you promote the welfare of the whole.**

Creating Connection in Everyday Moments

You can create connection by proactively identifying and appreciating moments to consciously find meaning in whatever you do—sometimes in the most unexpected ways, as I discovered after a grueling uphill hike.

Two major obstacles were preventing me from attaining my ultimate goal: the famous Potato Chip Rock photo op in my hometown, Poway, California. To get to the famous ledge, I needed to climb a huge boulder. Then, somehow, I needed to cross what seemed to be a bottomless ravine leading to the ledge. I studied the techniques of the other (much younger and fit) climbers. But with a recent knee replacement, I simply couldn't find a way up the big boulder. So I yelled from the base of the huge rock, "Is there a strong young man up there who could help pull me up?" A man crouched, steadied himself, and held out his hand. I couldn't reach it. Suddenly, I felt someone push me from behind. I grabbed the man's hand and found myself flying up the rock. But the ravine was another matter. The only approach was to jump across.

That's when I noticed a strapping young man straddling the ravine and lifting his terrified girlfriend to the other side. I boldly asked him, "If I take your photo, would you be willing to help me across? I can't make the jump." After I took his photo, people helped me slide into position, and he carried me across.

What happened next is the real lesson from the day. The configuration of the ravine made it impossible to get back across the way I'd come. A committee formed to figure out a solution. After several failed attempts, a man knelt, giving me his knee as a launching pad, as two men on the other side facilitated my crossing. And then, a chain reaction started. Each group coming up to the ravine began helping each other across. We all literally applauded our ingenuity. What had been a queue of hikers waiting their turn to cross the ravine for photos became a community finding more innovative ways to help launch and lift. The time between photos was shortened considerably.

Why did it take an old lady like me with an artificial knee to break the barrier of "I-have-to-do-this-on-my-own-without-help" mentality? Hundreds of hikers have reached the top of the mountain without having their photo on the famous ledge because they couldn't find a way to navigate the obstacles. Why are we so averse to asking for help? For some of us, the reason may be ego or fear of being vulnerable. But for most of us, it's simply that we're not aware of the beauty of being interdependent.

My Potato Chip Rock photo op was thrilling, but what I hadn't anticipated was changing the dynamic on top of the rock. The greatest thrill of the day was seeing people enthusiastically being of service. I've seen research proving the axiom that giving is more precious than receiving. On that rock, I saw it in action.

> **You can create connection through authentic relationships and a sense of belonging.**

When I see the amazing photos of me on Potato Chip Rock, I don't see me triumphantly alone on the ledge; I feel the support of my friends and a community who helped me get there. I learned that asking for help when you need it doesn't just increase performance. The wonderful irony is that when you ask for help, you not only experience an intense sense of gratitude for what you receive, but you also help others experience the joy of interdependence and contributing to something greater than themselves.

Are You Undermining Connection?

The World Health Organization recently declared addiction to video gaming as a global mental health issue. Video games can brilliantly (and deceptively) create choice and competence—every decision you make is a choice with immediate feedback that enables you to gauge your effectiveness, increase your competence, and move through levels. What video games don't usually do is help you create connection. The relationships formed in multiuser games tend to be superficial and competitive. To those who become addicted, gaming becomes a priority to the extent that not much else matters or feels valuable.

Games don't have to erode connection—game developers are learning that infusing games with meaning might be good for users as well as developers. But video games provide an example of how we can naively undermine connection without realizing it.

To avoid undermining connection, practice actions from the list below:

- Stop pursuing a goal for an external reward. Doing so diminishes the chances of finding a more meaningful and purposeful reason for pursuing that goal.

- Begin engaging in discussions to explore emotions and feelings—mine and those of others.

- Listen with an open heart.

- Don't judge—myself or others.

- Instead of accepting organizational metrics without meaning, find ways to attribute my own meaning to what my organization is asking of me.

- Align my work and goals to higher-level values or sense of purpose.

- Stop treating business as if it isn't personal—almost every decision and action at work affects my energy, income, opportunities, and future. How is that not personal?

- Speak truth to power—especially if it's on behalf of someone who needs an advocate.

- Be honest about my needs, fears, and vulnerabilities.

- Ask for help when I need it.

- Speak up against injustice and unfairness.

The prime minister of the United Kingdom appointed a minister for loneliness in January 2018, citing a study that claimed more than nine million people in the country often or always feel lonely—which can be worse for health than smoking fifteen cigarettes a day.[1] In the United States, over 40 percent of adults say they are lonely, which has been associated with a greater risk of cardiovascular disease, dementia, depression, and anxiety.[2] Over 50 percent of CEOs say they are lonely in their roles. Loneliness in the workplace has been shown to limit creativity, impair reasoning and decision making, and reduce task performance.[3]

If you've ever felt isolated, abandoned, rejected, regretful, hostile, vindictive, or without purpose or meaning, you know what it feels like to lack connection. Taking actions to stop undermining connection is important, but you can cut to the chase by asking yourself three questions to create connection.

Questions to Create Connection

Ask yourself targeted questions to create connection:

When it comes to my goal or situation,

1. Can it give me a greater sense of belonging or genuine connection to others involved?
   - If I feel a greater sense of belonging, why?
   - Could my active involvement contribute to the welfare of others?
   - Could this goal or situation lead to a bigger purpose? Why might that be important?

2. Is it meaningful to me?
   - If I find it meaningful, why? Are important values aligned to it?
   - When I think about the purpose of my role, do I see any connection between this goal or situation and my purpose? Why?
   - What is the impact if I don't get involved?

3. Do I feel what is being asked of me is fair and just?
   - If I feel it is fair and just, why?
   - If I feel it is not fair and just, why?
   - Is it worth standing up for given my values or purpose? Why?

These questions create connection. When your motivation depends on gaining status and power or being fearful of not meeting the expectations of someone important to you, focus on ways to create connection. If you find yourself not caring about someone or something, remember, the opposite of love isn't hate; the opposite of love is not caring. The only way to make up for a lack of caring is aligning your goal or situation with meaningful values, personal purpose, or work-related purpose.

We all long to experience a sense of belonging that is core to who we are as human beings and to do work infused with meaning.

You can deepen connection by thinking bigger. Focus on how you can build community and contribute to the greater good. Advocate for changes or improvements that promote justice and fair play.

Visit the *Master Your Motivation* page at www.susanfowler.com to learn more about creating connection.

5

.

Create Competence

To master your motivation, create competence. To create competence, you need to

- Feel effective at managing everyday situations
- Demonstrate skill over time
- Feel a sense of growth and learning

Competence reflects your need to grow and learn each day. A toddler incessantly asks, "Why?" Her basic nature is to learn. A child learning to walk is full of joy. He falls but gets up because he relishes learning this vital skill that will make him more effective in life. Creating competence can be exhilarating. I'll never experience the thrill of dunking a basketball off a fast break or kicking the winning goal at the World Cup, but I have been elated by writing a quoteworthy sentence or watching my Italian husband delight in homemade pasta sauce.

I was working with my colleague Dobie on a complicated project. Her eyes were bloodshot from days of analyzing data. I asked her if she was okay. She responded, "You know, I'm physically exhausted, but I'm also excited. Working on this project makes me feel smart." As it happens, Dobie is smart and competent at what she does—she had just accepted the fact for herself. She was effective at managing the day-to-day demands of the project. She was demonstrating real skill. She felt she was growing and learning. She was effectively creating competence.

> **You have an innate need for competence—to experience progress, gain mastery, and feel confident and resilient as you meet the challenges life can throw at you.**

Brett loved almost everything about his job until he met Sally. He dreaded dealing with Sally. He described her as experienced, smart, and high performing but also as a bully who insulted team members and created high anxiety during meetings. Brett admitted he was intimidated by Sally—which was problematic because he was her manager! With emotions flaring and excuses flying, Brett would hang up from calls with Sally feeling exasperated, exhausted, and embarrassed for himself at being so inept.

After taking a motivation workshop offered by his company, Brett readily admitted he needed to create choice and connection to improve the situation with Sally. To his surprise, it was after answering the questions to create competence when "the magic happened." Brett had begun to question his ability to lead—and it was affecting more than his relationship with Sally. He had to admit that he was lacking the skill to handle conflict and deal with an aggressive staff member. Brett successfully reached out for guidance to help foster a better working relationship with Sally.

What I found inspiring about Brett's story was how a high-level manager mastered his motivation by admitting his inability to deal with a situation. One of the most important aspects of creating competence is an openness to being coached. Studies on coachability show that no matter your job—sales, competitive athletics, or entrepreneurship—proactively seeking to improve your interpersonal and work-related skills is directly correlated with productivity and role-related effectiveness.[1]

Don't Be Fooled by Assuming Competence You Don't Have

Have you ever watched the auditions for a television singing competition? A contestant steps up to the microphone with total confidence. She is optimally motivated; after all, she enjoys singing and has been taking lessons to grow her skill. She truly believes she's a great singer because of all the praise she's received from family members afraid to tell her the truth for fear of crushing her dream. Admirable intentions. But as you listen to her audition, you wish someone had loved her enough to provide an honest appraisal.

Feedback doesn't have to kill dreams—in fact, it's essential for building skill and achieving your dreams.

As you might predict, the judges tear down the auditioner's performance. She can't believe it. Her competence has just been shattered—and she's in denial. When it comes to a specific goal or task, it's not enough to think you're skillful if you are not. To create competence on a specific goal requires more than feeling confident in your ability. At some point, you need to demonstrate competence.

Your competence is eroded when you don't see reasonable progress on your goal over time.

Competence doesn't necessarily equate to mastery. It depends on your goal. Maybe you haven't mastered the goal of schussing down black diamond ski runs, but you can create competence if you are effectively managing the bunny slope and focusing on what you learn so you see progress each time you ski down the hill. But your competence will ultimately erode if you're embarrassed or frustrated to still be snowplowing down the bunny slope after years of lessons and practice. If you haven't progressed toward your goal of skiing black diamond runs, chances are good that you'll give up even attempting to ski.[2] But if your goal is simply to enjoy being on the mountain, hang with your friends, and sip spiked hot chocolate beside the fire at the end of the day, snowplowing the bunny slope may be all you need to create competence.

Are You Undermining Competence?

To avoid undermining competence, practice actions from the list below.

- Stop emphasizing outcomes and short-term results over learning and growing.

- Don't discount or avoid training, instruction, and advice.

- Avoid focusing on my mistakes instead of lessons learned.

- Develop the mindset and skillset of a self leader who proactively asks for the direction and support I need to achieve my goals.

- Remember that perfection is the enemy of progress.

- Ignore outside criticism that I'm not up to the task—unless it's legitimate feedback for getting up to speed on the task.

- Craft an action plan for achieving my goal that includes a learning plan.

- Cease comparing myself to others and judging myself as inferior. Instead, use information about how others are doing as data that informs my learning plan.

- Never assume competence—if I haven't demonstrated I am able to do something, open my mind to learning something new.

Don't underestimate the power that comes from being able to manage your everyday life with effectiveness. Marie Kondo is living proof of this power. Her book on the life-changing magic of organizing, folding, and cleansing—or tidying up, as she refers to it[3]—has sold over seven million copies worldwide with over eight thousand five-star reviews on Amazon! She makes reorganizing your closet and drawers meaningful: keep only the items that spark joy. But what makes people giddy is learning how to fold everything from socks to shirts and store them vertically. (If you don't believe me about the giddiness, ask me about my scarf bins.)

Motivation science explains the success behind Kondo's approach. Her lessons on how to make meaningful decisions about what "stuff" to keep, donate, or toss create choice and connection. But the magic happens when you learn the skills necessary to organize your space, sparking the joy of creating competence.

If you've ever felt inferior, ill-equipped, inept, scared, fearful, frustrated, or impotent when it comes to your goal or situation, then you know what a lack of competence feels like. Taking actions to stop undermining competence is important, but you can create competence by asking yourself key questions.

Questions to Create Competence

Ask yourself targeted questions to create competence:

When it comes to my goal or situation,

1. What skills or experience do I have that might prove helpful?
   - What core competencies can I draw from to manage the challenges I face?
   - Why are drawing on my skills, experience, and core competencies important?

2. What new skills could I develop?
   - What progress have I made in my skill development?
   - Why is developing skills and making progress important?

3. What insights have I gained—or might I gain—that could help me moving forward?
   - Why is moving forward important to me?
   - Have I made mistakes? Why is learning from my mistakes meaningful?
   - What have I learned that will help in the future?

These questions create competence. When your motivation is suboptimal because you feel overwhelmed or inadequate, focus on appreciating what you might learn from the experience or pursuing your goal.

We all long for the opportunity to grow, demonstrate resilience, and gain wisdom from our experience.

Create competence by learning from your mistakes and then sharing your wisdom with others.

Motivation
Is a Skill

One of my personal goals appears to be common around the world, if the money spent on diets and losing weight is an indicator. For years, I tried all kinds of tricks to lose weight, eat healthy, and exercise. I willed myself to avoid junk food but failed. So to alleviate the need for willpower, I created a "supportive environment." I threw out all the junk food and stocked my cabinets with healthy choices.

As popular books recommended, I disciplined myself to document my eating and workout habits. I even joined a group where we tried to excite each other by awarding ourselves tokens and points and held each other accountable with weekly weigh-ins. Despite the pressure I felt to lose weight and adopt healthy habits, I couldn't resist fast food (especially fried chicken with biscuits and gravy). All the willpower in the world couldn't make me get rid of the pot of pork fat on my stove because everything tasted better cooked in pork fat. Or so I believed.

One evening, I happened to catch a television news report about how we treat the animals we eat. Fifteen minutes later, I knew I would never eat meat again. I have not eaten meat or fish—or foods containing them—for almost forty years. From the outside, I appear to have amazing willpower or enviable discipline. But becoming a vegetarian required no willpower or discipline. I wasn't even excited about becoming a vegetarian. Searching to understand what shifted my motivation in those fifteen minutes—and has sustained it for almost forty years—led me to the science of motivation and a bold realization. Motivation is a skill.

The skill of motivation includes three actions, shown in figure 2, to generate and maintain the optimal motivation you need for achieving your goals.

Figure 2   The three actions in the skill of motivation

A chapter is devoted to each of the actions, but before you delve into the skill of motivation, select a goal to work on. Pick a persistent problem where you need a breakthrough (such as smoking or weight loss) or a routine task that is affecting the quality of your work experience (such as expense reports). Select a goal or situation where you feel blocked, are procrastinating, or aren't progressing as you wish. Or choose a goal where your motivation depends on an external reward such as a prize, bonus, or incentive—or an intangible reward such as power, status, or enhanced image.

An intriguing target for practicing the skill of motivation can be a character flaw you have tolerated in yourself for too long that needs a permanent solution, such as exaggerating the truth or not listening. Do your team members complain about something you are doing or not doing—such as cancelling one-to-one meetings or talking to upper management about getting more resources? You could choose a chore or project you haven't handled that frustrates friends, family members, or coworkers.

Listen to what you complain about but do nothing to address, such as a goal you think was unfairly imposed on you that leaves you feeling resentful. Challenge your motivation on a great idea you haven't had the courage to act on yet.

Are you ready to put the first action to work? If you're not sure, maybe you could practice with this task: read this book and put one idea into practice over the next two weeks. Whatever topic you choose to use as your personal example, I hope you learn to master your motivation on a worthwhile goal.

6

Identify Your Outlook

Two aliens crash-land in Minnesota, smack-dab in the Mall of America. Studying the complicated, multitiered map showing the layout of the mall's five hundred stores, they find the location of an electronics store where they can get the parts they need to repair their spaceship. They've traversed the galaxy but have no idea how to navigate one of the largest malls on the planet. Then they spot a red dot labeled "YOU ARE HERE." They plan their route. But they get lost along the way, so they find another map, locate their destination, spot the red dot, and recalibrate their route. That's when one alien turns to the other, scratches his head, and says, "That red dot is amazing. How does it always know where we are?"

No matter what journey you're on, you need to know where you are before you can decide the best way to get where you're going. That's why the first of three actions to master your motivation is to identify the type of motivation you have right now, as shown in figure 3.

Motivation science has verified six different ways of being motivated, called *motivational outlooks*. Each outlook has distinct characteristics that either create or erode choice, connection, and competence. The six outlooks are reflected in the Spectrum of Motivation model shown in figure 4 and the inside back cover of this book.

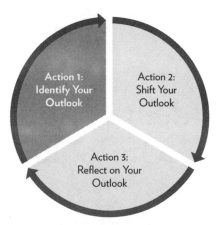

Figure 3   Action 1 in the skill of motivation—
identify your outlook

Notice that three of the outlooks, the disinterested, external, and imposed outlooks, reflect motivation lacking
choice, connection, and competence (low-quality psychological needs). When a suboptimal outlook describes the type
of motivation you have for your goal, you are less likely to
achieve your goal. But even if you did achieve it, you are less
likely to experience positive energy, vitality, or well-being.

On the other end of the spectrum, the aligned, integrated,
and inherent motivational outlooks reflect motivation satisfying choice, connection, and competence (high-quality
psychological needs). When an optimal outlook describes
the type of motivation you have for your goal, you are more
likely to achieve it. But even if you don't achieve your goal,
you are more likely to experience positive energy, vitality, and
well-being.

**You are always motivated. The question is,
What type of motivation do you have?**

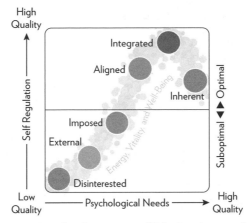

Figure 4   The Spectrum of Motivation model

Keeping your goal or situation in mind, use the descriptions below to identify which of the six motivational outlooks best describes what you are currently experiencing. Don't be surprised if you find more than one!

Three Suboptimal Motivational Outlooks

Does one or more of these suboptimal outlooks describe your current motivation?

Disinterested Motivational Outlook

When it comes to achieving my goal or resolving my situation, the reason for my motivation is

- I don't care.
- I am too overwhelmed.
- I don't have the energy to manage what's required.

External Motivational Outlook

When it comes to achieving my goal or resolving my situation, the reason for my motivation is

- I have been promised a tangible reward or incentive.

- I expect that it will bring me power, an enhanced image, or status.

- I hope that I will receive people's love or respect.

Imposed Motivational Outlook

When it comes to achieving my goal or resolving my situation, the reason for my motivation is

- I want to avoid damaging a relationship with someone who has expectations of me.

- I have feelings of guilt, shame, or disappointment in myself.

- I feel pressure. I have to do it. (I fear what might happen if I don't.)

Three Optimal Motivational Outlooks

Does one or more of these optimal outlooks describe your current motivation?

Aligned Motivational Outlook

When it comes to achieving my goal or resolving my situation, the reason for my motivation is

- I am able to demonstrate important values.

- I derive a sense of meaning.

- I've made a conscious and deliberate choice to do the right thing.

Integrated Motivational Outlook

When it comes to achieving my goal or resolving my situation, the reason for my motivation is

- I feel a deep sense of purpose.

- I feel I'm being the person I want to be.

- I'm tapping into a conscious but almost automatic way of being.

Inherent Motivational Outlook

When it comes to achieving my goal or resolving my situation, the reason for my motivation is

- I'm having pure fun and enjoyment.

- I have an unexplainable interest in and attraction to it.

- I have always gravitated to it naturally.

Looking Deeper into the Suboptimal Outlooks

Anya's goal was to earn an MBA degree. After studying the six outlooks, she was surprised to discover her reasons for going back to school were all over the spectrum. Some days she felt like giving up—balancing work, family, and school was overwhelming (disinterested outlook). Other days she dreamed of the prestige, respect, and status the degree offered (external outlook). On other days, she felt the pressure of pleasing her parents who had prodded her for years to get her degree and then join the family business (imposed outlook).

One thing became clear as Anya considered the reasons behind her motivation to earn an MBA: they were all suboptimal. No wonder she'd procrastinated on taking the steps necessary to achieve her goal! By identifying her motivational outlook, she took the first action toward mastering her motivation—and perhaps earning a master's degree.

As you work on a goal as your learning example, you will probably have a few aha moments about other goals.

You will come to appreciate how a suboptimal outlook kept you from achieving a goal in the past. If you sense you have a suboptimal outlook for your goal, the descriptions below will help you understand why.

The Disinterested Motivational Outlook Is Debilitating

When you hear yourself complaining about your motivation, you probably have the disinterested outlook: "I simply don't care," "I'm overwhelmed," "I don't have the energy to deal with this." When you have the disinterested outlook, you cannot find any good reason to exert energy. You are just going through the motions.

Have you noticed how not exercising makes you more tired but working out makes you feel energized? The same is true about working on your goal when you have the disinterested outlook. Ironically, not having the energy to work on your goal or situation can be exhausting! You find yourself needing pick-me-ups throughout the day just to make minimum progress. Your vitality and well-being are at risk. Not creating choice, connection, and competence makes the likelihood of achieving your goal slim.

There are as many reasons for having a disinterested outlook as there are goals. Maybe you've been assigned a project you simply don't care about. Maybe you are an introvert who prefers alone time and your job requires you to attend networking events. Maybe you're exhausted keeping up with major changes in the workplace. "I'm just running in place until it's over" is how a young man explained how he was handling changes at work.

Living in ambiguity and uncertainty is challenging for many of us. But withdrawing from the situation, not caring about it, or putting your head in the sand and hoping it blows over doesn't benefit anything or anyone, least of all your own health and well-being.

Having a disinterested outlook for one goal is bad enough, but what if you're disinterested in your job, a relationship, or life in general? A motivational outlook can color your whole world in negative ways (or, if optimal, in positive ways).

If you have the disinterested motivational outlook, you expend enormous amounts of emotional labor, effortful self-regulation, and brainpower to compensate for your lack of choice, connection, and competence. Other areas of your life may begin to suffer because you simply don't have enough positive energy to cope.

> You have a disinterested motivational outlook when the reason behind your motivation eludes you, you find no value or good reason to be involved, or you are so overwhelmed by the situation that you have given up. This outlook doesn't provide any opportunity to create choice, connection, or competence.

The External Motivational Outlook Is Enticing

Pursuing your goal for the lure of a reward can prove seductive. Expectations that achieving your goal could bring power and status or enhance your image with others are tempting. The promise of winning people's love and respect along with your success is appealing. But like a poisoned apple or fool's gold, these reasons for your motivation are deceiving.

The external outlook distracts you from creating choice, connection, and competence. External rewards have been proven to replace more meaningful reasons for pursuing and achieving your goal—and can prompt unethical or questionable behavior in pursuit of the almighty prize. While you may gain competence when motivated with the external outlook, chances are, you won't notice because your focus is on winning, not on learning. You will find that your performance is easily compromised—like a basketball player who keeps his eye on the scoreboard instead of the ball in play.

The external outlook can trick you into believing that rewards compensate for being miserable. Imagine you work in a call center. The moment you take a customer call, a timer starts. Your goal is to complete the call within a certain time—before a red light starts blinking. Your focus is on the number of calls you service in a day rather than the quality of the service you provide. The warning light, the pressure to meet a quota, and the inability to consistently meet the demands of rude or angry customers are the ingredients for a goal devoid of choice, connection, and competence. That's when you turn to other reasons for pursuing your goal—such as money, incentives, getting attention or praise, or receiving people's admiration. No matter what your goal, your motivation is suboptimal when you declare, "It's a good thing I'm getting paid to do this: otherwise, I wouldn't do it."

When under the spell of the external outlook, you give up control of your motivation and place it in the hands of those who can decide to—or can decide not to—bestow power, status, love, respect, or tangible rewards to you. You are doomed to be at the mercy of others and fall prey to their opinions.

A participant in one of my workshops shared what she said was a trivial but relevant example. That morning, she had selected a new blouse to wear to the course. During our conversation about suboptimal motivation, she shared, "I was sitting here feeling sad, and I couldn't understand why until you explained the external outlook. I realize now that my motivation for wearing the blouse was to impress all of you. But when no one commented on how nice I looked, I doubted myself and felt inadequate. Over a silly blouse! Now I understand that the external outlook is dependent on people's opinions that I can't control. My energy and attitude were influenced by what you thought about my blouse! How silly is that?"

A woman in the class remarked, "That's so funny, because the first thing I thought when I saw you this morning was how lovely you looked in that blouse! I just didn't tell you!" Then a young man raised his hand and said, "I was going to tell you how flattering the blouse was on you, but I was afraid of how it might be interpreted. These days, you're not sure what's appropriate and what's not, so it's safer to just not say anything!" The case of the woman in the lovely blouse may have seemed trivial, but she learned a huge lesson about the nature of the external outlook.

> You have an external motivational outlook when the reason behind your motivation is to gain tangible rewards such as money and prizes, or intangible rewards such as power and admiration. This outlook erodes your psychological need for choice because you don't control the rewards. You risk eroding connection because the rewards distract you from finding more meaningful reasons for pursuing the goal.

The Imposed Motivational Outlook Is Irritating

The imposed outlook seems to pop up during the day more than any other outlook—especially for people who wake up feeling imposed on. Some people wake up thinking it's a glorious day, eager for the wonders that lie ahead. But others wake up wondering what challenges they'll need to conquer and what obstacles they'll need to vanquish. Some are more of an optimist, some more of a pessimist (or, as they prefer to think of it, a realist who shows up fully prepared for battle).

Whether you are inclined to be imposed on or not, the most telltale sign of the imposed outlook is pressure: "I have to do it because I'm afraid of what might happen if I don't."

For example, you call a business meeting and send out the meeting invitations, and when the day comes, you mumble,

"Dang, I have to go to that meeting." Your mind has interpreted the time blocked out on your calendar as nondiscretionary time—a symbol of having no choice. Ironically, you called the meeting, yet you still feel pressured by a lack of choice!

Pressure can be a driving force even if we're not aware of it consciously. Barry had survived a vicious layoff at a Texas oil company. He and his coworkers told me poignant stories of how they were relieved to have a job but also carried the fear of future layoffs and "survivor's guilt." Barry and others accepted positions beneath their ability or work they didn't enjoy so they could hold on to their jobs. When I asked them during a class to identify their current motivational outlook for their situation, everyone identified a disinterested or imposed outlook, as I expected. So I was surprised when Barry was the only one who identified an aligned outlook.

When I expressed my uncertainty over his choice, Barry became strident in his defense. "I may not like the job or the situation, but I said I'd do it and, by golly, I will!" he exclaimed. I asked him if he felt pressure and some resentment having to do a job that was beneath his skill and that he didn't like. "Yes," he admitted, "but when I say I'm going to do something, I do it!" Barry explained that his motivation was aligned to his value of finishing whatever he starts. While I agreed that motivation based on an important value would indeed reflect the aligned outlook, I pointed out that his feelings of pressure, resentment, and potential guilt for not keeping his word sounded more like the imposed outlook. Barry refused to budge.

Thinking I must not have understood Barry's true feelings or that I'd not expressed my point effectively, I asked if we could chat over lunch. I asked Barry where his value of always finishing what he starts came from. He answered without hesitation: "My parents were adamant—don't start something if you aren't going to finish it." Now I was faced with a delicate situation that caused me to hesitate. Barry was an obese man. Was there a connection between finishing everything he starts and being overweight?

"You know, Barry," I treaded lightly, "you might want to investigate that value more thoughtfully. Are you sure that everything you start is worth finishing? Could it be the better part of valor to recognize when a path isn't taking you where you want to go? Maybe a meal doesn't have to be finished to provide the nourishment you need. Sometimes, after setting a goal, you discover it isn't worth pursuing." After a pregnant pause, Barry buried his head in his hands, mumbling to himself. Finally, he looked up and revealed what I'd thought to be true.

Barry agreed to address the class after lunch. In an emotional confession, Barry explained that he had come to understand how he'd been living with a value that wasn't his but his parents' value. He had never truly thought about what it means to finish what he starts. He realized now how his unexplored value had affected everyday decisions, contributing to his weight gain over the years. He'd lived with the pressure of someone else's expectations—eroding choice, connection, and competence. Barry expressed relief in identifying his imposed outlook because it explained so many mysteries. By completing the first action of identifying his motivational outlook, he could now move forward to master his motivation for his work and his physical health.

> You have an imposed motivational outlook when you lack choice because you feel you "have" to do something. You lack connection because deep down, you resent the person or persons responsible for imposing their will on you or blame yourself for letting yourself down. You lack competence because of your inability to control your fear, anger, pressure, shame, or guilt and deal effectively with your feelings of being imposed on.

SCIENCE SAYS

If you love or value what you are doing, you might think that adding incentives or rewards could only make it better. An entire industry is devoted to rewards programs based on the belief that external rewards (suboptimal motivation) plus optimal motivation equals übermotivation. Not true. When it comes to motivation, one plus one equals less than two.

I wrote Edward Deci, the father of intrinsic motivation research, for his expert opinion on claims that combining extrinsic and intrinsic motivation maximizes your motivation. He responded by stating that a definitive meta-analysis on the use of external incentives and rewards clearly proves that extrinsic and intrinsic motivation are *not* additive but *negatively interactive*.[1] According to Deci, another definitive meta-analysis shows external incentives can predict the *quantity* of performance, but optimal motivation predicts the *quality* of work.[2] He explained that in a work setting, the use of pure sales commissions led to the highest level of turnover of any study that has ever been published in organization psychology literature.[3]

Are people motivated by money? Yes. By rewards, power, and status? Yes. But these types of external motivation are inferior because they don't create choice, connection, or competence—in fact, they have a proven undermining effect.[4] Bad motivation spoils good motivation. Motivation science may not be magic, but casting off the enchantment of the external motivational outlook can feel magical. Keep in mind, magic isn't magic to the magician.

Looking Deeper into the Optimal Outlooks

This is not a "workbook," but here is one exercise I encourage you to do using pen and paper or electronic notes. Take thirty seconds to make a list answering the question, Who am I? Go beyond your name, job title, and obvious role as a brother, sister, parent, grandparent, spouse, partner, aunt, or uncle. Consider roles and activities related to your work, hobbies, sports, or leisure time, such as people developer, financial analyst, team builder, amateur golfer, dog lover, church volunteer, cat aficionado, charity leader, wine connoisseur, television watcher, community activist, or property manager.

Look at your clock. Ready? thirty seconds. Go!

Now evaluate your list. Chances are, some of your roles involve activities you'd do even if you weren't paid. You make time to do them. You find them meaningful, integral to how you define yourself, or joyful and pure fun. In other words, your list probably includes goals and activities that reflect all three optimal outlooks—aligned, integrated, and inherent. So, how do you make the distinction among the optimal outlooks? The differences are worth noting because each outlook has its pros and cons.

- The aligned outlook is consciously chosen based on the value represented by the goal or activity: *I practice martial arts because I value health and fitness.*

- The integrated outlook is consciously developed, but it has become almost second nature, so it doesn't feel as conscious. Your motivation is based on a sense of purpose that has become internalized—it's one of the ways you define yourself: *I am a martial artist.*

- The inherent outlook isn't consciously developed but stems from a natural intrinsic interest. Your motivation is based on your enjoyment of the activity itself, regardless of value or purpose: *I enjoy the martial arts; I always have, but I can't tell you why.*

Why are these distinctions important? Here's an example. My friend Brent has an inherent outlook for playing a well-known video game. He plays when he can, like during a break or when eating a meal by himself. It's fun. He truly enjoys it. But sometimes he finds himself slipping into almost an obsessive desire to play the game—it's so much fun, it's hard to stop playing. How can Brent stop playing the video game and use his time more productively?

All three optimal outlooks reflect choice, connection, and competence, but just because an activity is inherently or intrinsically motivating doesn't mean it's worth more time than an activity based on meaningful values and a noble purpose. By being aware of the goals and activities where he has an aligned or integrated motivational outlook, Brent can choose when to have fun, create meaning, or seek both. If you sense you have an optimal outlook on your goal or an item from the list you created, consider which outlook best describes your motivation.

The Aligned Motivational Outlook Is Authentic

When a deeply held value becomes your primary reason for pursuing your goal, you have the aligned motivational outlook.

With this outlook, you consciously and deliberately choose to do the right thing—to be authentic to your values.

If your goal is to lose fifteen pounds by the first day of summer and I ask you why, your answer will reveal your motivational outlook. An answer such as "To look good for my school reunion" probably reflects an external outlook. An answer such as "Because my doctor put the fear of God in me—if I don't lose weight, I'm a candidate for a heart attack or stroke" reflects an imposed outlook. (If you thought about going on a diet but are ambivalent—you don't really care one way or the other—you probably have the disinterested outlook.)

But an answer such as "I want to lose weight because I value health and well-being," based on a consciously chosen value, likely reflects an aligned outlook. The more your goal is aligned to core values, the more authentic you are.

The beauty of the aligned outlook is that you create choice because values are conscious choices about what you deem right and wrong, good or bad. You create connection because values reflect what you find meaningful in your life. And you create competence because values provide the guiding light for making good decisions and feeling effective.

The problem with the aligned outlook? You need to know what your values are! Some values are programmed, but developed values are most effective for creating choice, connection, and competence. A developed value is

- *Freely chosen.* When a value is freely chosen, it hasn't been coerced or forced on you. The value wasn't embedded by cultural forces without your participation. You have freely questioned the source of the value and trust that the value is valid and appropriate for you.

- *Chosen from alternatives with an understanding of the consequences of the alternatives.* For a value to be consciously chosen, it needs to be weighed against other alternatives. Most programmed values have been internalized without consideration of the options.

- *Acted on over time.* All developed values have a behavioral component. A developed value is backed up by your behavior over time. While exceptions may occur, saying you value something but not acting on it is a major contradiction. For example, your credibility as a leader is at stake when you say you value teamwork but reward individual performance over team effort. Your employees, students, and children will not regard you as a values-based leader if your actions are self-serving and betray the values you say you hold.[5]

▪ *Prized or publicly owned.* A developed value can stand the light of day. You may not relish having one of your values announced on the evening news, but do you really value something if you can't share it with your loved ones? In a work setting, declaring a value allows you to test your value in light of others' perceptions—giving you a chance to examine possible alternatives and anticipate consequences. This can also be uncomfortable. Have you ever worried that coworkers would discover you agreed with a decision your boss made, fearing they'd consider you a traitor? Have you ever bitten your tongue during a conversation, afraid of how people might judge your opinion? Prizing a value publicly allows you to test your emotional attachment or conviction to it.

A wonderful example of developing a value is Gandhi and his vegetarian lifestyle. Gandhi was raised as a vegetarian in India. As a young man, he noticed that the British, who were the ruling class, ate meat. Perhaps this was the source of their power, he reasoned. One night, he and a friend pilfered some meat and, in a secret tryst, ate it.

Even though he became violently ill, Gandhi continued to eat meat, hoping to experience the strength and vitality that he believed was required for his people to overcome British tyranny. After years of experiencing an alternative to being a vegetarian while studying and living in countries outside of his own, Gandhi came to realize that eating meat had nothing to do with the political issues that were the source of his passion. He reconsidered his values on the matter, understanding the consequences of both alternatives.[6]

Finally, returning to India in 1915, Gandhi began his famous nonviolent revolution. As he "fought" for Indian independence, he *chose* to become a vegetarian, reflecting not only his culture's values but what he'd learned about animal rights while studying in London. Gandhi's story is a wonderful example of moving from a programmed value (being a vegetarian without conscious thought) to exploring his beliefs (trying meat) and *choosing* a developed value (evolving from animal rights to human rights).

You will learn more about values—including generational programmed values—throughout this book. For now, I hope this point is clear: you cannot fully experience the aligned outlook without developed values.

> You have an aligned motivational outlook when your motivation is a conscious choice to align with meaningful and developed values that reflect something other than pure self-interest. This outlook creates choice because you are making a values-based decision to act. You create connection because your goal is aligned to meaningful values. You create competence because you feel effective at living life on your terms.

The Integrated Motivational Outlook Is Internalized

The name of the next outlook says it all. When you have an integrated outlook on your goal, you perceive that achieving your goal is essential to how you define yourself. For example, if you have an integrated outlook to be healthy, then eating well and exercising reflect who you are—it's what you do.

If for some reason you gain weight, you can tap into the way you define yourself for your motivation to eat and exercise differently. Your self-concept supports your weight-loss goal: "I am a fit person; I'm athletic; I cherish my body because when it's healthy, I am better able to do the work I'm meant to do; I am an energetic model of health and well-being." Recognizing your self-identity may be all you need to revert to positive eating habits.

You can develop an integrated outlook in two ways. One way evolves over time. For example, in the introduction to part 2, I described my becoming a vegetarian. I developed a value about the way we treat animals after seeing a news report. With an aligned outlook, I consciously stopped eating meat. Sometimes I slipped into an imposed outlook when I was hungry and couldn't find a vegetarian option, but my values were reinforced through my conscious expression of choice, connection, and competence. Over the years, not eating meat became second nature to me. Today, I have an integrated outlook: one of the ways I define myself is "I'm a vegetarian." My integrated outlook is deep-rooted—I don't need to consciously remember not to eat meat. I don't necessarily love being a vegetarian. I just am one.

The second way you can experience an integrated outlook might come in a flash from a profound moment of insight or after experiencing a significant emotional event. That's what happened to Lee, a former Marine and bona fide tough guy. When he discovered his son was gay, Lee was judgmental and not as supportive as he could have been. Shortly after coming out, Lee's son committed suicide. The suicide note he left behind rocked Lee's world to its core.

As Lee processed his loss and his behavior, he became more outspoken about the issues his son faced. Today, Lee's life work is speaking to children, educators, and adults about bullying, signs of depression, and symptoms of withdrawal.

He speaks about inclusion, love, and embracing differences. Lee's motivational outlook is integrated—his work on behalf of his son's legacy has become a part of who is and how he defines himself. Lee certainly wouldn't describe his work as fun or enjoyable, but he derives lasting and meaningful rewards by fulfilling a deep-rooted sense of purpose through his advocacy.

Both the aligned and integrated outlooks result from conscious choices you make based on values or a sense of purpose. An integrated motivational outlook for your goal offers the greatest potential for achieving that goal and more importantly, for generating meaning in your life.

> You have an integrated motivational outlook when the reason behind your motivation is to fulfill a deep sense of purpose or is so second nature that it reflects how you define yourself. This outlook creates choice because you are making a purposeful decision to act. You create connection because your goal is connected to a deep-rooted purpose or reflects your self-identity. You create competence because you are effectively living life on purpose.

The Inherent Motivational Outlook Is Intrinsic

When you have an inherent outlook, you're intrinsically motivated to achieve your goal. You don't need a reward, good reason, or excuse to do what you are doing. You proceed for the fun and enjoyment of it. You may not be able to explain why you're interested or attracted to the goal—it's something you've always gravitated toward. You easily get into a "state of flow" where time flies and you have no idea where it went. You might find yourself "in the zone," generating positive energy and creativity. Abundant research proves the glory of pursuing a goal when you have intrinsic motivation.[7]

Sounds great, but chances are, one of these nagging problems prevents you from experiencing the inherent outlook as much as you'd like:

- Intrinsic motivation is rare—especially at work. (How often during your day do you say, "I'd do this even if I wasn't getting paid"?)
- You don't know what intrinsically motivates you.

To help identify and nurture the inherent outlook, begin by looking backward. Most of us discovered our intrinsic motivation early in life. Remember what you loved doing as a kid on a carefree Saturday morning or summer day.

I remember hearing a story from one of my favorite public speakers, Lou Heckler (his real name!). While he was rummaging through boxes of childhood memorabilia with his mother, they came across his report cards from grade school. Almost every teacher had commented, "Lou talks too much." Lou said to his mom, "Aren't you glad I didn't pay attention to their criticism? Today I get paid to do what I love—talk!"

What have you always loved to do for the simple enjoyment of it, even if the reason you love doing it is a mystery to you? Can you identify at least one activity that you loved as a child that you still make time for as an adult?

If you are still struggling to identify activities where you have an inherent outlook, notice what you gravitate toward when you have time on your hands. Edward Deci has long lamented that we overprogram our lives, robbing ourselves of the discretionary time to be bored. Deci knows that the truth about motivation is that no one wants to be bored, so we find ways to entertain ourselves. And that's when we discover our inherent motivation—what we enjoy doing simply because of our intrinsic interest in doing it.

Next time you have an unplanned moment, leave it that way. Keep an empty space on your calendar without an expectation of how you are going to fill it—even if it's thirty minutes. Then notice the activities you gravitate toward. Do you want to bake a cake, build a bookshelf, paint, sing, dance, or read? Recognize your yearning. Your downtime can reveal the things you are intrinsically motivated to do and help you take advantage of an inherent outlook in the future.

> You have an inherent motivational outlook when the reason behind your motivation is a fun mystery. You enjoy what you are doing but aren't sure why. A goal easily captivates you. This outlook creates choice because only you can decide what you enjoy doing. You create connection because while pursuing your goal, you are following your bliss. You create competence because your ability to achieve your goal matches the challenge and requirements for achieving your goal—the balance between your interest and ability generates a natural state of flow.

Identifying your motivational outlook is the first action for practicing motivation as a skill. Simply noticing your motivational outlook can be a mindful moment that prompts an automatic shift to an optimal outlook. But as you will discover in the next chapter, learning to proactively shift your outlook is a powerful act that can dramatically improve the chances for achieving your goals—and the quality of your life.

Discover more about identifying your motivational outlook by visiting the *Master Your Motivation* page at www.susanfowler.com.

7.

Shift Your Outlook

Shifting from suboptimal to optimal motivation—the second action in the skill of motivation, shown in figure 5—is inspiring!

Gratefully, people who have experienced shifting agreed to share their stories. Some agreed to let me represent them—and I sought feedback until they approved the accuracy of their experience. Others wrote their own stories, which are presented in their own words.

> **Shift happens when you proactively create choice, connection, and competence.**

The shifting strategies revealed through the diversity of stories are designed to do one thing: illustrate the wealth of opportunities and resources and the variety of ways you can shift your motivational outlook on your own goal by creating choice, connection, and competence. I hope you'll find important insights—and hopefully inspiration—in each example to help you shift your own motivation.

Notice how the questions to create choice, connection, and competence described in chapters three, four, and five

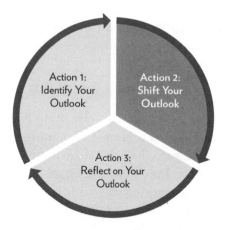

Figure 5   Action 2 in the skill of motivation—
shift your outlook

have been used directly or adapted by people to help them
shift their motivation and achieve their goals. As a reminder,
these are the questions simplified to their essence:

1. *Choice:* What choices have I made and what choices
   can I still make?

2. *Connection:* How can I deepen connection through
   demonstrating genuine caring, aligning with my values
   and purpose, or contributing to the greater good?

3. *Competence:* How can I build competence by acknowledging my skills, developing expertise, and learning
   something new?

As you follow the stories and examples for shifting, you
might find it helpful to refer to the Spectrum of Motivation
model in figure 4 (also shown on the inside cover of the
book). The model is descriptive—it depicts the six motivational outlooks that reflect different types of suboptimal and
optimal motivation. But it is also prescriptive—it shows how

to shift between suboptimal and optimal outlooks according to the quality of your self-regulation.[1]

Shifting out of a Bad Habit

Roland was a lifelong smoker. He grew up in North Carolina and was the son of tobacco farmers. Smoking was a part of his life—he would have felt guilty if he didn't smoke! Inevitably, his doctor gave him stern warnings to quit. He knew he should quit; the glaring warning on the cigarette package was a constant reminder. He tried, but since he was burdened with an imposed outlook, his efforts were futile. He chewed stop-smoking gum; he wore a stop-smoking patch. But he continued to smoke, got horrible nausea, spit out the gum, and pulled off the patch. He signed up for stop-smoking classes—and found himself grabbing a cigarette during the break. He quit (the class, not smoking). He heard about an acupuncture point on the ear that reduces cravings, so he had his ear pierced. Nothing worked.

One day, he was driving his car, smoking a cigarette, when his three-year-old daughter cried out from the backseat, "Daddy, please quit smoking. You're killing me back here!" It took a moment for her outcry to sink in, but when it did, Roland experienced an immediate shift. He realized that smoking violated two of his primary values: his daughter's health and being a good role model. He put out the cigarette and never smoked again.

Roland reports that to this day, he's surprised how easy it was to stop smoking when he made a values choice that enabled him to shift from imposed motivation to aligned motivation. As he says, "I chose to love my daughter more than the cigarette."

Roland created choice by realizing he had the power to smoke or not smoke. He created connection by recognizing

70

> **Giving up a bad habit may be as simple as loving something you value more than you love the bad habit.**

that he loved his daughter more than anything else in the world—and being a good father was his most important role. He created competence by taking a step in being a good father, not to mention mastering a bad habit he'd tried to give up for years. When you create choice, connection, and competence, you also create courage—the courage to take action for the right reasons.

Roland's story highlights a critical issue that surfaces if you want to shift from an imposed to an aligned motivational outlook. You cannot align to values if you don't know what your values are—which raises the question, How do you know what you value?

What Do You Value?

To begin exploring your values, try this experiment:

1. Make a list of five to ten of your general life values. For example, family time, health and well-being, financial security, compassion for others.

2. Now, evaluate your stated values against two questions:
   - How do you spend your money?
   - How do you spend your time?

These two questions reveal the veracity of your stated values—they expose whether your values are fully functioning in your life or you talk a good game. For example:

▪ Your value statement is "I value work-life balance." But the reality is, you spend sixty-five hours a week at work, often choosing business matters over family matters, and expect the same of your team members.

- Your value statement is "I value innovation." But the reality is, you don't spend time nurturing people's creativity but rather applying pressure to drive results that shut down people's creativity.

- Your value statement is "I value compassion—I really care about people." But the reality is, you donate less than 5 percent of your income to charitable causes, and you don't donate time to help the less fortunate.

- Your value statement is "I value health." But the reality is, you bought a gym membership and don't use it.

Your answers disclose discrepancies between your espoused values (what you say you value) and your developed values (what you act on). Shifting from suboptimal to optimal motivation is nearly impossible if you are fooling yourself about what you value. How will you stick to a diet if you say you value health but really don't? How will you donate to a worthy cause if you say you care about people less fortunate but really don't?

Ironically, other people probably know more about your values than you do. People judge your values through your behavior and deeds. They notice how you spend your time and money. Research shows that people use their judgment of your values to conclude whether you are worthy of friendship, if you are a servant leader or a self-serving leader, and whether you can be trusted to act on what you say.[2] If they see you as self-serving and untrustworthy, you are also seen as less effective—as a leader or an employee, a friend or partner.

My friend Deborah had a novel idea for evaluating a potential online dating candidate. She said, "I wish I could just ask him for his credit rating, the type of car he drives, and his BMI [body mass index]."

For Deborah, the young man's credit rating could provide insight into his values concerning responsibility or financial security. The car he drives might point to values such as status or environmental concerns. His BMI could reveal values regarding health.

Even though Deborah was joking, she tapped into a powerful idea. Research shows that more than race, gender, or generation, the most important criterion for forging meaningful relationships is a match in values.[3]

But values hold the key to more than relationships. When you align your work-related goals to values, you attribute meaning to your work. When you align personal activities to values, you gain fulfillment in even the most mundane moments.

Comparing your espoused values with how you spend your money and time provides potent insight into your values. I encourage you to expand on the basic exercise to develop values for yourself. But you may also need to consider where your values come from in the first place.

If you are about to eat a bunch of french fries, you might think twice if you ask yourself what you value more than french fries—such as your health and well-being. If you are about to send a nasty email because you think someone made a boneheaded decision, you might hesitate if you ask yourself what you value more than being right—such as building the relationship rather than destroying it. If you are about to work overtime again, you might reconsider your priorities if you ask what you value more than the money or power you are working for—such as having dinner with your family or tucking your kids into bed.

Aligning with values to shift your motivation requires distinguishing between your espoused values—and your developed values. If you haven't deeply thought about which of your values are espoused or developed, if you aren't sure where your values come from, maybe it's time to investigate.

Where Do Values Come From?

A developed value is an enduring belief that a particular end (your desired outcome) or means (your desired way of achieving your outcome) is more socially or individually preferable than another end or means. Notice a key word in the definition of a value: *belief.*

> **The quality of a value is determined by the quality of the source of the belief behind the value.**

All your values come from underlying beliefs. So to understand where your values come from, begin with your beliefs. For example, when your beliefs are tied to an expert or authority—whether it's a religious leader, the *New York Times*, or your parents—your beliefs are only as solid as that authority. When doubt is cast on the source of your beliefs, your derived beliefs are cast in doubt. Fallen role models and discredited authority figures often cause a values crisis—or should!

Challenging your beliefs—and especially the sources of your beliefs—has never been as important as it is in today's world of fake news. The veracity of what we see and hear needs to be challenged, especially on social media. But on any newsstand in the world, you can see magazines and newspapers announcing bogus weddings, events that never happened, and conspiracy theories. We need to be vigilant about the sources of information that underlie the beliefs we form. Those beliefs, based on truth or not, result in the values that shape how we live, who we vote for, and decisions we make in every facet of our life.

To examine where the beliefs that shape *your* values come from, ask the following questions:

1. What are my values?

2. What beliefs underlie these values?
   - When, where, and how did these beliefs arise?
   - Are they based on my experience?
   - Did they come from my parents? Family members? Friends? Social or religious groups? The military?
   - Did they come from another source or authority?
   - Have my beliefs been validated by others?
   - Have I ever challenged my beliefs?

3. What might I believe if I let go of this belief and adopted another?

4. Would my values shift if I considered a different belief? If yes, then how?

You owe it to yourself to validate your values by first exploring the beliefs that spawned them.

Not all beliefs are values, but all values are beliefs.

The good news? Values are personal choices. Begin to explore the beliefs and values you currently hold. Proactively develop values you act on and cherish by making conscious choices about how you want to live your life. Then keep those values in mind as you shift your motivation to give up a bad habit or embrace a new habit for something—or someone—more important. Aligning goals with values is a powerful way to generate positive energy and experience optimal motivation.

A business associate I greatly admire tends to live her life making values-based decisions—such as moving to a different country to pursue meaningful work. Yet Judith discovered that as well-intentioned as we might be, sometimes our personalities or desires can make it a challenge to live according to our values with an aligned outlook.

IN HER OWN WORDS Judith: A Journey to Integration

I found myself smack in the middle of Sam's personal cycle of drama. I wanted to avoid the gossiping that Sam instigated in our group but confess that I was sucked in by the drama. Even though I was a coconspirator, I would complain to my husband about Sam and what was happening with the team. My husband, a former police officer, could see right through my façade of blaming Sam for all the turmoil.

Around this time, I learned about the skill to master my motivation. Using this situation as a test case, I tugged at identifying my motivational outlook. At first, I identified with a disinterested outlook—saying I just didn't care about Sam's problems. But then I realized my emotional reaction to the ongoing situation didn't reflect disinterest. The telltale signs were my feelings of resentment and anger over the time being wasted hashing out Sam's latest crisis. I also had to admit that the reason I engaged in the gossip and drama was an unhealthy need to be liked by others and seen as being "in with the group." I finally identified my imposed outlook.

I decided to see if I could shift my motivation for dealing with Sam's gossiping from suboptimal to optimal. I asked myself the questions to create choice, connection, and competence and came to three realizations:

1. I had choices. I could choose to get embroiled in the dramas or not to engage in the gossip.

2. I could connect to my values. One of my strongest values is honoring time. Gossiping, complaining, and getting wrapped up in someone else's drama was not honoring precious time. If I acted on my values and refused to get involved, I was choosing to use my time more meaningfully.

3. I could build competence by focusing on what is productive rather than trivial and shallow.

I became more mindful of my options. I excused myself when the gossip started, explaining to the group that I didn't feel comfortable talking about a person without them being present to share their side of the story. I became more judicious about the activities I agreed to participate in with the group. I was remarkably energized by aligning with my value for honoring time.

But I also discovered that sometimes mastering my motivation on one issue leads to an unexpected shift on another issue. By standing up for team members when they were the targets of gossip and not present to defend themselves, I deepened my connection to them. Perhaps even more surprising, my lifelong need for acceptance paled in comparison to the positive sense of well-being I felt protecting the integrity of others. Even

continued

more profound, my noninvolvement halted the negative whirl of energy I had been contributing to the world.

Mastering my motivation, I went beyond honoring time to an integrated motivational outlook for fulfilling my stated life purpose to be a positive force in the world.

Judith's story not only demonstrates how to apply the skill of motivation but also reinforces how mastering your motivation takes you beyond achieving your goals. We have all fallen victim to social pressures that compromise our values and disconnect us from a more noble purpose. When you are mindful of being de-energized or energized by cruelty, unfair treatment of others, or other actions that run counter to your stated values and sense of purpose, you can identify your motivational outlook and take corrective action to shift your outlook by creating choice, connection, and competence.

What Does It Mean to Self-Actualize?

Mastering your motivation promotes living an authentic life with integrity. Mindfully creating choice, connection, and competence has proven to support the synthesis or integration of the desired behavior with other aspects of yourself—making you more wholly you. As a result, you are also more likely to find yourself not only creating choice, connection, and competence but living a life with a greater sense of well-being, vitality, and self-actualization.[4]

Speaking of self-actualization, Maslow's hierarchy of needs comes up almost every time I teach or speak on motivation. Maslow posed the idea that people are motivated by satisfying lower-level needs such as food, water, shelter, and security before they can move on to being motivated by higher-level needs such as self-actualization.[5] But the reality is, you can experience high-level motivation anytime and anywhere. Unlike Maslow's needs, choice, connection, and competence are not hierarchical or sequential but foundational to all human beings and our capacity to thrive.[6]

The exciting message for you is that you can experience optimal motivation anytime and anywhere you choose by creating choice, connection, and competence. Self-actualization is a lofty aspiration, but it's not a place you arrive, like the top of a mountain. Being self-actualized isn't a one-time goal to be accomplished. Rather, self-actualization is a process of maximizing your abilities and resources to mindfully greet and find meaning in everyday challenges and opportunities. Self-actualization is a *process* for becoming—it's never static. Mastering your motivation is the skill required for this process.

Phil has a zest for life that is unmatched. He is a minister, teacher, and entrepreneur who also has a passion for practicing the skill of motivation. He acknowledges that we all have issues that might keep us from being who we want to be—such as anger, impatience, jealousy, pessimism, indifference, resentment, and pride, just to name a few. Phil realized he had to shift his motivational outlook day to day to satisfy his need for choice, connection, and competence.

IN HIS OWN WORDS   ## Phil: Life Credo

"Mr. Reynolds, there is a 5 percent chance your current aneurysm will burst before your scheduled surgery." As the doctor was speaking, I could only think about the twenty-three days in the hospital when my

continued

first aneurysm burst in December of 2016. I did not want to experience another long stay in the hospital where I wouldn't be working or spending time with family and friends. I said, "Well that means there is a 95 percent chance it won't burst! I will choose to live in the 95 percent."

I wrote my credo to create choice, connection, and competence in the 95 percent:

- *I choose to always act with a purpose.* When you are not certain about the time you have left, you want to be sure that what you are doing is making a difference. Every action has some layer of intentionality behind it, whether it's taking my wife to dinner or tackling difficult issues with clients.

- *I choose to write a daily gratitude list.* Every day has something to be grateful for. Even on days when I feel physically terrible, I take time to reflect on the people, experiences, and things for which I am grateful. This gives me some perspective on who I am and the people who've changed me; it allows me, through the pain of my illness, to be grateful.

- *I choose to send thank-you cards or emails.* I take time to say "Thank you!" to the people who have made a difference in my life. Writing a physical note helps me reflect on the positive. As a bonus, it gives that person a positive emotion for their day.

- *I choose to stop complaining.* Complaining led me to negative thinking, which impacted not only my state of mind but my emotions. I must take ownership of my thoughts and actions to maintain my level of energy and focus. Complaining produces no solutions and solves no problems.

- *I choose to learn something new every day.* I read. A lot. I learn from my participants in workshops. I have mentors who answer my questions. I listen to my kids!

Mastering my motivation to live in the 95 percent with choice, connection, and competence improved my well-being and, I'm convinced, helped me heal. But more importantly, the quality of my motivation helped the quality of life for my family and close friends who went through this challenge with me every step of the way.

Phil's credo defines Phil in a nutshell. I am pleased, but not surprised, to report that after living in the 95 percent during multiple operations and rigorous rehab, Phil is back to 100 percent as a life coach and flying across the country teaching workshops on topics he knows from firsthand experience, such as self leadership and trust.

Craft Your Own Credo

You might want to follow Phil's lead by writing your own credo. The word *credo* is Latin for "I believe." A personal credo is a statement of your core beliefs, or guiding principles, and your intentions for integrating them into your everyday life.

To create an optimally motivating credo to help you shift when you feel overwhelmed by a situation, external distractions, or pressure, include actions that will help create choice, connection, and competence. For example, consider statements such as these:

- ■ I create choice:
  - • I choose how I wake up and live my life every day.
  - • My choices reflect my values and who I truly am.

- ■ I create connection:
  - • What I do to others, I do to myself.
  - • My work is meaningful and contributes to a greater good.

- ■ I create competence:
  - • I consciously improve my skills because doing what I do well is one of the ways I contribute to others.
  - • By learning something new each day, I spark wisdom, progress, and change.

You are never too young to consider your life credo. Ivan is working full-time to put himself through college. I think his story is a perfect example of how by creating choice, connection, and competence every day, optimal motivation becomes a conscious and deliberate act.

IN HIS OWN WORDS

Ivan: A Credo in the Making

I'm not a morning person, but I get up at 1:30 a.m. to work delivering snack food to grocery stores at 3:00 a.m. The older guys I work with teased me—asking me, "What's a young guy like you doing here?" They thought I should be in school. They were surprised when I told them I *am* in school. I'm a full-time student in my junior year as a political science major. As soon as I'm done with my eight-hour (or longer) shift, I attend classes between 3:00 p.m. and 10:00 p.m., depending on the day.

One day, my manager called me into his office. I was afraid he'd learned I was working and attending school full-time and would force me to make a choice. But it was just the opposite! He told me, "I never thought school was important. I just wanted to earn money. Now I have a wife and two kids, and I have to work. But because I don't have a degree, options are limited. If I had it to do over again, I'd have stayed in school. So, if there's anything I can do to help you, let me know. We can rearrange shifts to accommodate a test or doing your homework. What you're doing now will affect the rest of your life. Make the most of it. Who knows? Maybe you'll inspire me to go back to school."

I was blown away. His words reinforced the decisions I'm making. Over the years, I've learned about the skill of motivation. When I am faced with a decision, I create choice by asking myself about the choices I have. I know I could choose not to go to school or work seven days a week. I accept responsibility for choosing to get my education and contribute financially to my family, who have always encouraged me to get my education.

I have learned to create connection by asking myself how I can find meaning in my goals and contribute to something greater than myself. I'd like to think my goals are based on values that I've thought about deeply. I don't feel driven to work hard—my motivation isn't because my parents or society pressure me. Some of

continued

the guys at work, and even my own friends, ask me if I resent the long hours or lack of sleep. But I explain that I'm choosing to work hard while I'm young and strong so I can earn my law degree and become a politician. I have seen firsthand the corruption in my parents' home country of Mexico and the misunderstanding of the complex immigration issues here in my own country. I'm dedicated to helping bridge different perspectives. I want to fight injustice for those less able to do it for themselves.

I create competence by asking myself, What have I learned that is important for my future? I try to listen to people who are willing to coach me—like my older sister, my parents, and mentors like Susan and her husband, Drea. After my boss shared his story with me, I shared it with Susan, telling her what I learned: people are willing to help you succeed when they see how hard you work. People want to help people who help themselves. Now I want to work harder, not just for myself, but because working hard to achieve my dreams might spark someone to achieve their own.

As well as anyone I know, Ivan reflects on his experience, learns lessons, and internalizes the lessons into a life stance. Talking to Ivan, I always come away from the conversation knowing more about him and *myself*, because his hunger for insight is contagious! His stories paint a picture of a young man creating a credo of proactively making choices, connecting choices to meaningful values, and building competence through experience. Perhaps developing your own credo can help you master your motivation and generate the positive energy to achieve your goals and live your dreams.

The Magical Combination

The psychological needs, choice, connection, and competence, can be measured individually, but they are deeply intertwined. For example, if your manager unfairly micromanages you and you don't deal with it, choice is eroded because you're being told what to do, how to do it, and when. Your connection to your boss is eroded because he appears oblivious to your needs. Your competence is eroded because your manager obviously doesn't think you can handle your work without his intervention—and creating competence when you doubt your ability to do your job is nearly impossible.

Over her career, Brenda's capacity to master the demands of her job had propelled her into a major leadership role in a prestigious company. Brenda's story demonstrates when one of your needs is out of whack, the others are diminished, and so is your optimal motivation. But when choice, connection, and competence are combined, they work like magic.

IN HER OWN WORDS **Brenda: A Magic Combination**

I dreaded the two-hour webinar to teach me how to use a new sales analytics tool. The only good thing, the meeting was virtual. My imposed motivational outlook was based on my fear of what might happen if I didn't attend (no choice). I also resented how these webinars interfered with more important and meaningful work (no connection).

continued

Working through the questions to create choice, connection, and competence in hopes of shifting my motivation, I was surprised by what I discovered. My "issue" wasn't about creating choice or connection, as I thought it would be. My suboptimal motivation was a lack of something I always prided myself in having: competence.

I tend to overlearn material. I follow a defined process for learning that I developed in college. I apply this process to everything I need to learn, holding myself to incredibly high standards. Now those high expectations were putting me under pressure. My process had failed—I was in over my head trying to master sales analytics tools.

Answering the questions to create competence, I "remembered" that while I was a seasoned veteran in my industry, I was new to this company. I had the perfect reason to opt out of using the complicated analytics tool until I was more grounded in other aspects of my work.

I had fallen into a trap of my own making by holding myself to unrealistic expectations in the face of competing priorities at this stage of learning a new role. Ironically, I wasn't creating competence—I was destroying it! Worse, my lack of competence had eroded choice and connection.

To shift my motivation, I created competence by accepting that I wasn't ready for the analytics tool—it "cluttered my head." Then I considered my options and realized I could create choice by speaking to my manager, clarifying my priorities, and asking for help to master the tool when the time was right. This way I could focus my energy on creating competence where it most mattered in my role.

Creating choice and competence gave rise to another aha moment—how to create connection that had been nonexistent. I recognized how much I admired and appreciated the techniques the instructor used to teach complicated concepts in a virtual setting. What if I changed my goal from learning how to use the analytics tool to a goal of improving my own teaching skills? By learning techniques to help me eventually teach the skills to my team, I would also learn to appreciate the analytics tool for its overall value in the sales process.

The questions to create choice, connection, and competence didn't reveal their answers in the order I asked them. But when I recognized my issue with competence, the others fell into place. Now I have an aligned motivational outlook to learn through teaching. But perhaps my biggest breakthrough is that by mastering my own motivation, I can teach my team how to create choice, connection, and competence for themselves.

Brenda discovered that shift can happen when you create choice, connection, and competence. But if shifting strategies haven't worked in your case, don't despair. Hold the hope of optimal motivation by taking the third action: reflect on your outlook.

Learn more about shifting your outlook by visiting the *Master Your Motivation* page at www.susanfowler.com.

8

.

Reflect on
Your Outlook

Creating choice, connection, and competence increases your
sense of well-being. Reflecting on your outlook heightens
your awareness of just how good optimal motivation feels!
Motivation science confirms that creating choice, connection, and competence feels so good, you want more—not
less. Mindfully feeling good makes you want to continue feeling good. You realize

- You have created choice—and can initiate more

- You have created connection—and can develop more

- You have created competence—and can build more

But reflecting, the third action in the skill of motivation as
shown in figure 6, also proves helpful if you haven't shifted
or you discover you have a suboptimal outlook.

Months after attending a motivation workshop I conducted, Josie, one of the participants, told me, "I was sitting
at my desk when I noticed my stomach was tied in knots. I
was feeling pressure and almost sick." That was when Josie
says the skill of motivation kicked in. She explained, "I
reflected on my motivation and identified I had an imposed
motivational outlook for a meeting scheduled later that day.
As I peeled away the layers to understand where the pressure

Figure 6   **Action 3 in the skill of motivation—**
reflect on your outlook

was coming from, I realized it was a coworker who would be in the meeting. She pushes all my buttons. I was anxious and worried about having to deal with her."

Josie continued, "I decided to see if I could shift my motivation. I considered my choices. I had choice—I could go or not go to the meeting. I'd chosen to go. I asked myself how I could create connection and realized the meeting was aligned to goals that were important to me and I could also live one of my values—being a team player. And then, like a time bomb going off when I least expected it, I got in touch with how it would feel if I could handle my coworker with grace instead of being scared of her! It may sound corny, but I walked into the meeting feeling determined, uplifted, and purposeful."

As Josie finished telling me her story, I was struck by her conclusion: "In reflection, I know the results of the meeting were transformed because *I* was. My coworker and I may never be best friends, but we have both remarked on how proud we are of working so well together!" Remember how Josie's story started out with her reflecting on the pressure she felt? And her story ended with her reflection validating how her shift in motivation led to positive outcomes. Reflecting is essential to maintaining an optimal outlook—or shifting if you haven't already.

How to Reflect

Sometimes talking to yourself isn't crazy. Asking yourself questions and mindfully answering them is a form of reflection. The questions to create choice, connection, and competence described throughout this book are mechanisms for shifting to and maintaining optimal motivation.

But even if you haven't shifted yet, the questions become a powerful tool for reflecting—especially if you focus on the *why* part of the questions. For example, when it comes to my goal or situation,

- *Why* am I making the choices I am making? *Why* am I not making certain choices?

- *Why* is this goal or situation meaningful to me? *Why* isn't this goal or situation meaningful? *Why* do I hesitate to connect with the people involved?

- *Why* is gaining competence important to me? *Why* isn't learning from this goal valuable to me?

When engineers are faced with an electrical or mechanical failure, they ask five whys to get to the root source of the problem. Human nature is infinitely more complex, so you may need to ask yourself why more than five times to get to the root source of your motivation. The effort is worth it, according to research showing that answering the why question reveals "whether one perceives the goal-directed behavior emanates from one's self or, alternatively, is brought about by forces or pressures external to the self."[1]

The questions to create choice, connection, and competence probe your whys and prompt something even more profound in the process: mindfulness. You can draw from a myriad of techniques to help you reflect, but mindfulness stands out as the superior strategy.

What just happened to your motivation when you read that mindfulness is a superior strategy? Did the idea of mindfulness pique your interest, resonate as true, generate disinterest, or maybe even tap into a fear that mindfulness could conflict with a religious or spiritual belief you have? By simply answering the question about your reaction to mindfulness— noticing how it affects you emotionally, physically, intellectually, and spiritually—you are on the verge of practicing mindfulness.

> **Mindfulness is being aware of and attuned to what is happening in the present moment, free from judgment or impulsive reaction.**

Being aware of what's happening is something you do day in and day out. You notice the sound of a fan blowing, your stomach growling, people speaking on the phone, the room temperature, the taste of food. But the challenge mindfulness poses is being attuned without judging or reacting in the moment! The point of mindfulness is to free us from feelings, emotions, experiences, bias, prejudice, and preconceived notions that prevent new ways of perceiving our world.

Ellen Langer, who's been studying mindfulness since the early 1970s, insists that mindfulness is not much harder than mindlessness.[2] You don't need to meditate to be mindful, although meditation certainly enhances mindfulness. Rather, you simply need to notice new things without judgment. To see for yourself what Langer's studies have proven, think of something you would describe as distasteful—such as rap or classical music. Now, listen to it. If you don't like football, watch it. As you engage with whatever you find distasteful, notice five or six new things about it. Chances are, the more you notice about the activity, the more you come to like or enjoy it. Mindfulness enables you to be open to alternatives, options, and other possibilities. Within those possibilities lies optimal motivation.

To master your motivation, reflect by being mindful of

- Feelings

- Reasons behind your motivation

- New perspectives

Be Mindful of Feelings

Early in our relationship, I continually hounded my introverted husband with the dreaded question, How do you feel? Known for his thoughtful letters to family and friends, he presented me with a note that began, "You tell me I don't share my feelings with you enough. So, for your birthday, I thought I would tell you how I feel." My heart skipped a beat. Then I read the next line: "I feel fine."

My husband's note has become a running gag in our family, but he reminded me in a humorous way that incessant probing about someone's feelings can be discomforting—and shut the person down instead of opening him or her up. Reflecting on your own feelings might be uncomfortable, but being mindful of how you feel at any moment is essential for mastering your motivation.

An effective question to ask yourself is, When I think about my goal, how does it make me feel? However, *feelings* is an umbrella term that needs to be unraveled before it can be useful. What is a feeling? Begin by making the distinction between physical sensations and emotions. I learned the difference the hard way.

After studying kung fu for a few years, I begged my instructor, Kenny, to spar with me. I wanted to put what I'd learned into practice. Kung fu is primarily a form of defense, so Kenny was hesitant to spar, preferring to focus on the mental aspects of self-control. I pleaded. Finally, he agreed and helped me don protective headgear, pads, and boxing gloves. I was so excited! Within seconds, Kenny landed a ferocious side kick that moved me about two feet sideways. I wasn't hurt physically because of all the padding, but I let out a shriek and started flailing—attacking with punches and kicks, ducking and swerving—with no sense of what I was doing.

Kenny stopped, held up his hand, and instructed me to take off my gear. I was confused. We had just started. "Pull it off," he instructed. "You are not in control of your emotions."

Kenny explained that I had let my emotions rule my behavior. I needed to learn to separate my feelings, the physical from the emotional, or I would fail. Kenny taught me that a physical sensation is taken in through my senses—pressure, pain, a smell, a sight, a sound. An emotion is my interpretation or opinion of the physical sensation. My emotions tend to be based on past baggage, future expectations, or fears—but not on the present moment. By not being in the present moment and letting my emotions rule my behavior, I would easily be vanquished by my opponent.

The following week, I asked to spar again. I donned the gear, took a breath, and began. It didn't take long for Kenny to raise his hand and instruct me to pull off my gear. I was still controlled by my emotions. I was not mindful. The reality is, some people are more naturally disposed to be mindful than others. My personality type tends to be more spontaneous, quick to react, and judgmental—the opposite of the characteristics required for mindfulness! My sparring experience taught me I had a lot to learn—and not just about kung fu.

The skill to recognize a physical sensation and the emotion tied to it is invaluable when learning to master your motivation. Don't simply ask yourself what you're feeling. Ask yourself what you notice about your physical sensations. If you feel a negative sensation—I call it a physiological disturbance—pay attention. Your physiological disturbance is probably tied to an emotion you haven't explored. Try to identify that emotion.

For example, if I grab your upper arm and squeeze, you have a *physical sensation* of pressure—and if I squeeze hard enough, maybe even pain. Without conscious thought, you probably also have an *emotional response*. You might feel flattered that I chose to squeeze your arm. You may feel annoyed because I am stronger than you are. You may be unable to identify your emotion until you peel back the layers and recognize a feeling of discomfort stemming from when you were a child and your father grabbed your arm to control you from wandering off in a large crowd. You never realized until now that when someone grabs your arm, you feel controlled—and maybe resentful.

Use your physical sensations as your alarm bell that reminds you to mindfully investigate the emotion lurking beneath the sensation. Adam, a sales leader, had achieved success in his field by responding to his client's feelings but ignoring his own. His story is a good example of how recognizing our own feelings can prompt a motivation shift.

IN HIS OWN WORDS Adam: Releasing the Burden

I enjoy meeting new people. Good thing, because networking is an important part of my job as a senior sales leader. That's why I was stymied by my procrastination to contact "Mr. B," a referral from a coworker.

To deal with my suboptimal motivation, I followed the three actions. First, I identified my specific motivational outlook. It became clear to me that when I spontaneously meet and interact with people, I have an inherent outlook—I gravitate toward it naturally. But in the case of Mr. B, I felt pressure, guilt, and regret—all signs of an imposed outlook. The mystery was *why*.

The next action would hopefully help me answer the why and prompt a shift by answering questions to create choice, connection, and competence. My answers about my choices helped me realize I was glad I had the opportunity but not glad about putting it off. I also accepted that I was *choosing* not to follow up with Mr. B.

The questions to create connection took me deeper. I had planned to avoid protocol and contact Mr. B without reporting it to my manager because of self-serving reasons—should I ever decide to quit my job, Mr. B could be a valuable resource. I had to admit to myself that I was betraying my boss and organization—not to mention my own values.

I probed deeper into those values and how they related to this situation. I was able to align contacting Mr. B with three of my workplace values, including being of service. Sharing my expertise would benefit not only Mr. B but also his customers, who would be better off with our

continued

company's product. I also recognized how my value for developing and coaching people could be fulfilled by sharing my knowledge with Mr. B and turning that experience into a teaching moment for my sales team.

The questions to create competence were a no-brainer. I had the skills to effectively reach out to Mr. B. And by interacting with Mr. B, we would both be learning. I was intrigued with the idea of mastering my own fears and overcoming my procrastination and sharing the success story with my team.

I could feel myself beginning to shift, but it wasn't until I began the third action in the process that the shift took hold. First, I reflected on how I felt at the beginning of this process—recalling feelings of shame, regret, and frustration. Then, I reflected on how I felt after answering the questions to create choice, connection, and competence. That's when the shift happened. As soon as I acknowledged my feelings—both physical and emotional, the fears that had blocked me from taking action lifted. My shoulders and neck released. I felt physically and emotionally less burdened, lighter. I had a sense of relief. I felt excited and hopeful.

Being mindful of my feelings gave me the energy to commit to an action plan. I committed to following protocol, sharing my intentions with my manager, and meeting with Mr. B. I am pleased to report that acting on my commitment generated a whole new level of feelings. Yes, I could personally benefit down the road, but more importantly, I feel gratitude that my outreach to Mr. B will bear fruit for him, his customers, and my organization. And I have a great story to teach my team members about how mastering your motivation works.

Adam noticed his feelings, but instead of judging them, he took the opportunity to explore them, learn from them, and then let some go and embrace others. Being mindful of your feelings—physical sensations and emotions—helps you master your motivation by affording you the space to avoid an inappropriate (or programmed) response and to acknowledge and identify your emotions so you can choose a more meaningful and growthful reaction.

SCIENCE SAYS

Mindfulness as a tool for getting to the essence of your motivation almost always creates choice, connection, and competence. A meta-analysis of hundreds of mindfulness studies reports an impressive and growing body of research showing how mindfulness increases insight and adaptability, decreases attachment to detrimental aspects of life such as emotional and cognitive disturbances, enhances physical processes such as the immune system, and helps people with "integrated functioning." Mindfulness generates newfound clarity that provides greater flexibility and objectivity.[3] The world needs to pay more attention to the growing body of work on how mindfulness generates empathy!

But these findings are especially relevant to mastering your motivation. Through neuroscience, the researchers found a fascinating link between a mindful state and what occurs when one's psychological needs are satisfied—the two phenomena light up the same part of the brain. Mindfulness appears to be the most effective and direct route to creating choice, connection, and competence.

Be Mindful of the Reasons
behind Your Motivation

Dr. Ken Blanchard has often said any diet works if you stick with it. The problem is, we don't stick with it. Why is that? By now, you probably know the answer: diets undermine choice, connection, and competence.

When my husband decided to go on a diet, I warned him he was being lured by false promises. As most of us do, Drea thought he was doing something good. But research shows that even if you lose weight on a special diet, you gain it back quickly (over twelve weeks, on average). Worse, you typically gain back more than you lost and become so discouraged, you don't believe in your ability to lose weight in the future.[4] You may get sucked in to diets when your company's HR department offers rewards for losing weight or be enticed by the vision of being idolized by classmates at your school reunion, but chances are slim (excuse the pun) you'll succeed.

To protect Drea from the pain of failure, I asked if he'd be willing to practice the skill of motivation on his weight-loss journey. (I think he agreed from an aligned, not an imposed, outlook!) His journey is described below—along with tips for how you can benefit from his experience.

Action 1: Identify Your Outlook

Drea examined why he wanted to go on the diet and decided he had an integrated motivational outlook. One of the ways he defines himself is as an athlete. Over the years, playing organized sports wasn't reasonable, and the inactivity without a change in diet took its toll. He was eager to "be more authentic to himself." I double-checked: he wasn't going on a diet to please me or impress anyone else but to be more integrated with the person he believed himself to be.

When you identify your motivational outlook, be brutally honest with yourself. Acknowledge the real reasons for embarking on a diet. Is your motivation suboptimal? If you are dieting to impress or are hoping for a tangible or intangible reward, concede you have an external outlook. If you are dieting out of guilt or shame for being overweight or fear of someone judging you or not loving you, own up to your imposed outlook.

You may have an aligned outlook because you've linked losing weight to an important value such as being healthy, having the energy to do the activities you enjoy, honoring the body you've been entrusted to maintain, or being a good role model for your children (but only if you aren't imposed on and acting out of guilt or shame). You may have an integrated outlook if, as Drea did, you consider dieting and losing weight an activity that empowers your authentic self.

Action 2: Shift to or Maintain an Optimal Outlook

To kick-start his diet, Drea chose to see a diet counselor, who conducted weekly measurements, including percentage of fat loss versus muscle loss. He also answered questions to create choice, connection, and competence—and had some fascinating insights:

- *What choices did you make this week that you are glad you made, and what choices do you wish you hadn't made—and why?* I was glad I ordered a hamburger wrapped in lettuce with no bun and red onions instead of white onions in my omelet because they have fewer calories. These choices made me mindful that I can make all kinds of choices I hadn't thought of before.

- *How did you deepen connection? Do you feel a greater sense of belonging? Did you align with values or a sense of purpose? Are others benefiting from your diet?* Feeling that I have control over my choices also makes me feel that I have more control over myself—it reminds me of being an athlete, taking care of my body, and generating more energy. My choices deepen my connection to my authentic self. I'm eating less meat, and I think that's good for the environment—an important value for me. I am also getting in touch with how much I want to be healthy for my grandchildren—to watch them grow. That's a reason for dieting that I didn't consider when I started but has become more and more at the heart of why I want to eat healthy.

▪ *What skills do you have that have proved helpful? What have you learned? If you've made mistakes, what have you learned from them?* I learned *why* red onions have fewer calories than white onions (less sugar content). When I ordered the hamburger, I was about to order the french fries. But I learned that I can pay for a whole order but ask them to fill the carton only halfway. They think I'm crazy, but why tempt myself if I don't have to? I learned that it feels good to eat only a few fries. I also learned that I don't have to be perfect. If I have a day where I eat more than I need, I accept it and find myself eager to get back to a routine that generates more positive energy. Fitting into clothes I didn't think I'd wear again is just a bonus.

Action 3: Reflect on Your Outlook

Drea reflected throughout his diet experience. Mindfulness was integrated into all the questions and his thoughtful answers. He continues to notice physical sensations and related emotions essential for making good choices and learning how his body reacts to food and exercise.

If you are dieting, reflect on how you feel, what's become clear, and the reasons for shifting and continuing to eat healthy. Reframe dieting so that you embrace the energy you're gaining, not just the weight you're losing. Reflecting provides food for thought that will fuel your options for moving forward.

I am happy to report that Drea is no longer dieting—for all the right reasons! Through awareness, mindfulness, and continued reflection, Drea no longer considers himself dieting. He has integrated a healthy way of eating into his life. He discovered he really likes hamburgers wrapped in lettuce, he feels full after a healthy salad, and he can indulge in his Sunday-morning waffle because he's aware that it's a treat he's choosing and not a cheat that might cause shame or guilt.

If you choose to change your diet or embark on a weight-loss journey, ask yourself these simple questions:

- *How am I creating choice?* When you are hungry and tempted by something unhealthy try asking yourself, "If I could have anything in the world, what would I have?" When you give yourself the freedom to make even an imaginary choice, you find yourself making the best choice.

- *How am I creating connection?* I have seen countless examples of people being unsuccessful at losing weight until they linked their efforts to values and a noble purpose that are more important than eating the food that leads to weight gain, less energy, or ill health.

- *How am I creating competence?* What you learn as you change your eating habits is often more fulfilling than what you're eating.

In chapter 2, I made the point that needing to use discipline could be a red flag warning for suboptimal motivation. If you need discipline to diet, you probably haven't shifted to optimal motivation. But when you shift, the result of your day-to-day behavior is discipline! Drea found his successful weight loss experience tapped into the discipline he felt as an athlete. Developing discipline through dieting with optimal motivation is totally different than having to be disciplined to diet.

Mastering your motivation is the key to solving the mystery of why diets don't work for losing weight—and what does.

Be Mindful of New Perspectives

Reflecting can help you shift your motivation when you're under pressure by providing fresh perspectives on everyday goals or routine tasks. Mark's experience is one most of us can relate to—no matter the goal. Mark and his wife, Siri, bought a home originally constructed in the late 1950s. Problems popping up weren't a matter of *if* but *when*. Mark admits that handyman duties are not his thing, so his solution was to outsource home maintenance. But over time, his strategy proved too expensive. He needed to change his approach—and that meant changing his motivation on home maintenance.

IN HIS OWN WORDS Mark: New Perspective on an Old Problem

Being on the road constantly for work, I found my motivation for household maintenance bounced back and forth between the disinterested and imposed motivational outlooks. A big issue was yard work. I just didn't care (disinterested) until people started complaining about the yard (imposed guilt and shame). But the last thing I wanted was to come home from a long road trip to mow the lawn and trim bushes.

Of course, I felt justified in my suboptimal motivation. But in hindsight, my outlook made me even more defensive. One day Siri, being the enlightened one, asked me, "Why do you enjoy doing the laundry so much?" As I reflected, I realized that I took pride in taking a big basket of dirty clothes and transforming it into a pile of neatly folded garments. I liked taking on a project with a beginning and an end—seeing it through to completion. Siri suggested that maybe maintaining the lawn could be like doing laundry. Wouldn't an overgrown yard bring me the same satisfaction as the pile of clean clothes? With Siri's vivid comparison, even I could see the connection. I felt myself begin to shift.

I went to Lowe's hardware and asked one of their experts to show and tell me how to use the best equipment and tools. Now I was gaining momentum—and creating competence.

But what sealed the deal was reflecting on my values and life purpose. This may seem like a stretch, but I realized how yard work connected to my life view around wellness! I have earned multiple black belts in the martial arts, am a certified yoga instructor, and have taught fitness for years. What if I could reframe mowing the lawn and trimming hedges into an outdoor workout? Today, I have an integrated outlook for doing yard work because I connect it to how I define myself in terms of my mental and physical health and fitness. Mowing the lawn isn't just something I do, but it reflects who I am. Who knew home maintenance would come to this?

Mark learned how to reflect on a goal he was optimally motivated to do (laundry) and use the insight to bring fresh perspective to a goal he wasn't optimally motivated to do. Mark had much to gain and little to lose in trying to shift his motivation. His negative energy, guilt, and defensiveness had been a burden. But is it worth the effort to shift on a routine task you have no interest in doing? That was Calla's situation. She didn't have negative energy—she was simply apathetic about expense reports. Typically, she waited until the last minute until someone "pushed her."

IN HER OWN WORDS

Calla: Reframing a Routine Task

Jenny sent me an email, as she had in the past, asking about my expense report. As usual, it was late. It seems I was almost always late with my reports, or they were incomplete. My last report was missing some receipts, so Jenny had sent me a note asking for them.

As I read her latest message, I realized that not submitting my expense reports on time, or submitting them inaccurately, was costing Jenny a lot of time. I like Jenny, and I certainly value what she does. I also do not want to have anything I do (or don't do) make unnecessary work for someone else. On reflection, I realized I was making Jenny's work a lot harder, and that was not consistent with my values. Framing the situation like that helped me realize I wanted to submit the reports on time, and correctly. Realizing why this routine task was important helped me want to do it right. My perspective totally changed. I moved from an imposed to aligned motivational outlook.

I called Jenny and told her that I was setting a goal for myself to have 90 percent of my expense reports submitted on time and error free. I asked her to work with me and give me feedback if I started to slip. We became partners in my goal. And guess what? I have accomplished my goal—and because my values haven't changed, my motivation to continue honoring my commitment hasn't changed either.

Reframing the task of submitting expense reports enabled Calla to shift from the low-quality energy of the disinterested outlook to the positive energy of the aligned outlook. I could argue that as Calla continues to reflect on submitting expense reports, she might continue gaining perspective: she could shift to an integrated outlook as the routine task becomes symbolic of being a loyal corporate citizen and a demonstration of contributing to her workplace community.

Mindful reflection can reveal new perspectives that we can't see until our motivation shifts. Every time you learn something, your brain creates new neural circuits or alters old ones. But if you always do what you've always done, your brain simply follows old pathways. For example, if you walk through the park the same way every day, no new paths are created, but the old pathway is deepened—not just in the grass but in the neural pathway in your brain. Sometimes deepening pathways is helpful—habitual behavior deepens your neural pathways, which enables you to do some things without thinking. Have you ever driven home and realized you don't consciously remember stepping on the gas pedal, stopping at a red light, or turning on the street leading to your house? It's almost as if your car drove itself home.

However, deep pathways aren't helpful when your motivation is suboptimal—they perpetuate low-quality energy. But you can use mindfulness to lift you out of the negative neural pathway that has you feeling disinterested, dependent on external motivation, or imposed on by pressure or fear. Imagine taking a helicopter ride in your brain, rising above the neural pathways—or what might be called ruts—that limit your thoughts and actions.

Shifting your motivation blasts you out of complacency or negativity. But then what? How do you keep from being sucked back into the rut? Eileen, an expert in resilience, describes how mindful reflection raised her above negative patterns and provided her options for proceeding.

IN HER OWN WORDS   **Eileen: Maintaining an Optimal Outlook**

I was newly single with about $1,000 in the bank and my possessions in the trunk of a Camaro; the move from Florida to California was huge. I was lucky to land jobs where I discovered skills I didn't know I had and developed new ones. Luckier still, while working in a PR firm, I met and married my gift-from-God husband. But working in large publicly traded companies and handling multinational PR clients, I also learned how dysfunctional organizations can be.

Happy with him? Yes! Miserable at work? Yes! Interesting how finding joy in one part of your life can shine a light on how miserable you are in another part of your life. My job was not feeding my heart. I had no passion for getting some CEO on the cover of *Time* magazine or writing press releases for real estate developments. But here we were, not much money between us, and I turned to meditation, prayer, and asking for an answer. Two months into the marriage, in that half-awake state between sleep and the alarm, I clearly saw myself on the edge of a cliff and heard a voice say, "Jump. I will catch you." I sat straight up, punched Bill, and said, "I am quitting."

"What are you going to do?"

"I have no idea, but I can't do this anymore."

"Okay. We will always be all right." (See why I love him?)

Through reflection, I had become aware of what I didn't want. Quitting was indeed the start of an answer. How it would unfold remained a mystery. I continued reflecting and learned of an opportunity to create and deliver a three-hour seminar for a local college on "How to Write a Business Plan." I was reminded how much I enjoyed teaching. A random request led to another program, "The Art of Persuasion." Today, I continue to design workshops but also present before audiences as large as fifteen thousand and facilitate intense executive retreats as small as nine.

Mindfulness generated the awareness of options for moving forward that I couldn't have seen coming in my suboptimal outlook. I created choice by deciding to stop doing what doesn't feed my heart. I created connection by fulfilling my purpose of making a difference with the spoken and written word so that people discover their own possibilities to create a life of meaning. And I created competence by realizing that when I'm in the flow and experiencing the joy of "doing," I can't help but continue to learn.

Eileen's story reinforces that reflecting is the key for continuing to create choice, connection, and competence after you've shifted. Practicing mindfulness as a form of reflection keeps your mental helicopter aloft so you can keep rising above negative neural pathways in your brain. Eileen also learned that seeing the horizon from below the horizon is impossible, but new horizons emerge when you mindfully rise above the limited thinking that has you repeatedly following the same road instead of moving forward.

Through reflection, you realize that you can choose the quality of your experience anytime and anywhere. With practice, mastering your motivation shifts not only the quality of your motivational outlook but the quality of your life.

Gain more insight for reflecting on your outlook by visiting the *Master Your Motivation* page at www.susanfowler.com.

What's Stopping You?

My husband and I saw cars swerving erratically on the street we were walking down. A large tree limb had broken off, blocking a lane. Without saying a word to each other, we stepped into the street to pull the limb to the side of the road. But we couldn't budge it. We had no idea how heavy a tree limb could be! A man saw us struggling and joined us, but that limb wasn't moving. An oncoming car pulled over and a man jumped out, shouting instructions as he ran to the other side of the limb: "You're not going to get anywhere by pulling it, we need to push!" With all four of us pushing, we shoved the limb out of traffic.

The smart man climbed back in his car, the other guy went on his way, and as my husband and I went ours, we realized we were trembling. We had just risked life and limb (literally). Then we started laughing. We felt great! But our positive energy wasn't from an adrenaline rush. We felt high from the joy of collaboratively solving a problem. We'll never see those other guys again. And we'll never forget them.

We see glimpses of our true humanity in these kinds of spontaneous moments, when someone reaches out to lend a hand for no other reason than it's the right thing to do. A far more courageous and remarkable act of kindness and collaboration happened in Florida in 2017. I go back to watch the videos and read about the event time and again because it's such a wonderful demonstration of our true nature—and our need for connection.[1]

While swimming at Panama City Beach, eight adults and two young boys were swept away by powerful rip currents. Four of the adults were strong swimmers who had gone out to rescue the family and got caught in the deceptive currents themselves. With no lifeguards on duty and law enforcement opting to wait for a rescue boat, something had to be done. The eight stranded swimmers had been fighting the current for almost thirty minutes—they wouldn't last much longer.

Suddenly, volunteers on the shore, recognizing the dire situation, began forming a human chain. As the rescue mission became more desperate, dozens joined the chain. Two volunteers, Jessica and Derek Simmons, were strong swimmers. They swam along the chain to the stranded swimmers and began passing the children down the chain first, then the adults. The mother of the two boys passed out on the way back to shore from pure exhaustion and fear. She woke up on the sand, but the situation was dire. Her mother was still in the water and had suffered a heart attack. The older woman instructed rescuers to just let her go—save themselves, but they refused to listen. Barely able to keep their own heads above water, they held the woman up until Jessica and Derek reached them.

That's when the human chain grew longer and stronger. Eighty strangers linked wrists, legs, and arms to provide a path to safety for the ailing woman and the rest of her family. All ten of the stranded swimmers arrived back on shore to the applause of the entire beach. Jessica Simmons wrote in a Facebook post, "To see people from different races and genders come into action to help TOTAL strangers is absolutely amazing to see!! People who didn't even know each other went HAND IN HAND IN A LINE, into the water to try and reach them. Pause and just IMAGINE that."[2]

Revisiting the Panama City Beach story and my tree limb experience, I wonder why we wait for a natural disaster or a significant event to bring out our best. As human beings, we want to exhibit the positive tendencies of our human nature and we yearn for optimal motivation. What's stopping us from creating what we naturally long to experience—choice, connection, and competence? The answers to that question are explored in the next four chapters.

9

I Can't Shift

During a motivation workshop, managers for a major video game developer chose a goal where their outlook was suboptimal and then took turns asking one another the questions to create choice, connection, and competence. After twenty minutes, I asked everyone to get up and stand beneath the sign that represented their current motivational outlook. I was thrilled as participants moved to the side of the room where I'd placed signs for the aligned, integrated, and inherent outlooks! They had experienced a shift. Then I noticed Neal, Marty, and Louise standing on the suboptimal side of the room.

Neal manages the graphic artists who design some of the most popular video games in the world. But as a fine artist with a prestigious art degree, he felt his talent was wasting away in a world of cartoon characters. Neal's goal was to spend time painting in his preferred style. Ironically, his love for painting was a source of pain because he never had time to do it. His inherent outlook for painting had become suboptimal with feelings of guilt for not painting and anger at having so little time outside of work to pursue his passion. Going into the questioning exercise, Neal's outlook was clearly imposed.

But now Neal was standing under the disinterested outlook sign! He had shifted—but in the wrong direction. Confused, I asked him what happened. Neal explained, "After thinking about the choices I have, what is meaningful in my life right now, and where I can best learn and grow, I realized my job and family are my top priorities. I don't have time to work, spend quality time with my wife and kids, and paint. So I'm giving up the painting for now. It will come back into my life when I'm ready."

I interpreted what I heard Neal say: he was making a values-based decision to postpone painting because he found more satisfaction by focusing on his job and family than indulging his love of painting at this time in his life. He agreed, so I asked, "Describe your emotions with this decision. Do you still feel frustrated? Do you feel resentment, anger, or regret?" Neal replied, "No. I feel relief. Letting go of painting right now frees me up to enjoy my work and family more."

Neal's rationale made total sense, but standing under the disinterested outlook sign didn't. "Neal, you created choice by freely making a decision to postpone painting. You created connection by making that choice based on valuing your work and family. You seem to be saying that you can create competence in new ways. Are you sure your outlook for painting is disinterested, or are you making a values-based decision to postpone painting for now and proactively choosing your priorities?" He didn't say a word but walked across the room and stood under the aligned sign.

Suddenly, Marty practically ran across the room to join him, explaining as he went, "You just helped me understand that I was feeling imposed on by my goal to work out six days a week. But I can choose my work and family as my top priorities and work out three times a week without feeling guilty!" Of course, Neal and Marty always had the choices, but they had never reflected on their choices in light of their values and priorities.

Now Louise stood alone on the suboptimal side of the room under the imposed outlook sign. Her goal was to quit smoking after decades of nearly two packs a day. I could tell she wanted to walk across the room. I asked her how she felt about answering the questions and her current motivational outlook. She taught us all something about motivation in her response: "I thought I had a disinterested outlook to quit smoking. I always thought I just didn't care—that I was numbed after years of warnings from doctors, pleas from my family, and badgering by friends who had quit and couldn't understand why I hadn't.

"But after answering the questions, I realize that I'm afraid—afraid of getting cancer, dying, and disappointing my husband and children. I do care. I haven't shifted yet, but in my heart, I believe I will. The questions helped me face my fears. Recognizing my fears means I can begin dealing with them. I don't want to quit smoking out of fear or to please other people. I want to quit smoking because I've used my values to break through my fears. But that means I need to do more work on my values. After today, I am more aware of my choices, the connection between values for my health and my family, and my need to build competence for how to overcome this addiction."

Louise's confession was a poignant moment that left more than a few people teary-eyed. Her story reinforced how we don't always create choice, connection, and competence in the moment or spontaneously shift from suboptimal to optimal motivation. Sometimes mastering your motivation requires awareness that you have choices to make, connections to deepen, and competence to build—and then trusting that by practicing the skill of motivation, shift will happen.

115

Choosing Not to Shift

Gina, a district manager, had a good excuse for not shifting. In fact, she refused to shift. She was being held accountable to implement a new approach to selling that she vehemently disagreed with. After years of providing award-winning service to her customers, she was being asked to focus on upselling her customers instead of meeting their needs. Worse, she was expected to hold her team accountable for following the new policy. To say she had an imposed motivational outlook is an understatement. Asking questions to create choice, connection, and competence during a motivation workshop landed with a thud.

It became clear: she was feeding on self-righteous indignation—that red-hot energy that fires you up when you know you are right and *they* are wrong. The only way to sustain this insidious form of junk food motivation is to continue fueling the flames of negative energy through blaming, name-calling, and comparing your intelligence or status favorably to theirs. Gina justified her suboptimal motivation by recounting examples of how moving from values-based selling to a profit motive was already damaging long-term client relationships.

But to Gina's credit, when she reflected on how sad and deflated she felt, she realized she wasn't saying "I can't shift"; she was admitting "I don't want to shift." She acknowledged that she had chosen not to shift. Her honesty provided the openness to ask herself, "Why haven't I shifted?" and entertain the questions, "What if I did shift? Do I have any values that could support a shift?" Reflecting on these questions gave rise to a mindful moment and to intriguing possibilities. What if she was wrong? What if she could learn something? Gina had already expressed that learning, exploring new ideas, and being open-minded were important values.

116

With her newfound awareness, Gina announced to every-one in the class—including her sales team, "I just shifted. I'll either learn that I am wrong and they are right. Or I'll learn from experience what doesn't work and be a more effective advocate against the approach." She decided to embrace the new approach, full steam ahead. Her conclusion: "Either way, we all win."

Is It True?

Gina's experience of reflecting on her reasons for not shift-ing reminds me of Byron Katie's brilliant process of inquiry to question the thoughts at the root of suffering, called "The Work."[1] Katie asks you to answer four powerful questions when you have a negative judgment or conflict about some-one or something:

1. Is it true?
2. Can you absolutely know that it's true?
3. How do you react, what happens, when you believe that thought?
4. Who would you be without the thought?

After you answer the four questions, Katie asks you to turn your negative judgment around—to find one or more oppo-sites—and consider whether that turned-around thought or those thoughts could be true. Without her realizing it, Gina's reflection had revealed answers to Katie's questions: Is it true that this new sales approach is bad? How do you know it's true? Being open to the possibilities, Gina recognized the benefit of exploring the idea further. She'd either gain data to support the truth of her assertions or learn that she was wrong and fulfill her value for learning. Left with only constructive reasons for shifting, Gina could let go of her negative energy and focus on moving forward with positive energy, vitality, and well-being.

I'm not sure whether the scientific approach for shifting your motivation described in this book supports Katie's spiritual approach or vice versa, but I'm inspired by both. When I first experienced The Work, I was brought to unexpected tears by the question, Who would you be without that thought? I had gone to Barnes & Noble simply to hear Katie speak because I was impressed with the oversized postcard promoting her book signing that I'd received in the mail. As an author about to release a new book, I wanted to investigate good marketing schemes. I'd never heard of Byron Katie, but I had heard of her husband, Stephen Mitchell, a renowned author and translator of spiritual texts, who would be introducing her. I was intrigued.

I arrived early because I love wandering through brick-and-mortar bookstores. I was flabbergasted that a large crowd had already formed, taking every available seat within the cordoned-off area. Who were these people? I dragged a big stuffed chair across the store and positioned myself away from the groupies—for that's what I considered them. Like devotees of some weird cult, they were buzzing about their experiences with The Work.

I will confess now that I was terribly jealous. I was an author, had spoken around the world, had ideas that I thought could change people's lives—and though I'd never heard of Katie, plenty of people obviously had. They were raving about her. I grew suspicious. Seeing people so giddy made me wonder what was up. My judgments continued as Katie took the stage. She seemed nice enough but certainly wasn't the dynamic guru I was expecting.

Katie asked us to identify someone who makes us angry, upset, or sad. She gave us a form to complete called "The Judge-Your-Neighbor Worksheet." I happened to be frustrated and disappointed with someone in my life at that moment.

Then Katie began doing The Work. She asked a young man to share his story; then kindly, compassionately, and without judgment, she asked him, "Is it true?" He answered, "Yes." As Katie asked the young man her questions, I was silently answering them for myself. She gently probed, "Can you absolutely know that it's true?" Even though I was quite sure my judgments were true, I found myself with a smidgen of doubt. That little bit of daylight was all I needed. The door was opened for me to answer honestly and authentically the third question: How do I react, what happens, when I believe that thought? I was surprised by the negativity unleashed by my answer—heaviness, hostility, and hateful energy rushed through me.

Then the most miraculous thing happened. Katie asked, "Who would you be without that thought?" That's when I cried—not just a little tear but a deep and cleansing bunch of tears. The burden of judgment became so apparent to me that I no longer wanted to carry it. I wasn't tearful from sadness or regret but from relief!

I had gone to Barnes & Noble to see an author in action. I left loving the person I'd been judging so harshly. (Over a decade later, my positive feelings remain, by the way.) I also left with an admiration, appreciation, and understanding for the significant spiritual event that put Byron Katie on her life's path and her generosity for sharing what she learned through that experience. I encourage you to visit Katie's website, The Work, to learn more about how "to identify and question the thoughts that cause all your suffering."[2]

That day, I left with one more gem. I had clarity on how the science I'd been studying for years was aligned with Katie's spiritual approach. I recognized how reflecting on my judgments and letting them go satisfied all my psychological needs and shifted my motivation for working with an individual I had convinced myself wasn't worth the effort. I realized I could choose to hold on to the thoughts creating a rift between me and another person, or I could let go of my judgment. I chose to let go. My choice reinforced my connection to my better self—and to the person I was judging. It reinforced that I had the competence to self-regulate and generate positive energy—not only for myself but for those who were caught up in my judgment and negative vortex. My needs for choice, connection, and competence were satisfied.

That afternoon, I became even more intentional about translating the science of motivation for everyday application—primarily in the workplace but also for achieving personal goals. Remember, your natural state is to thrive. You cannot thrive when you carry a backpack full of junk food motivation—you suffer mentally, physically, psychically, and spiritually. When you find even a little opening to relieve that suffering, crawl or burst through it. Optimal motivation—and peace—awaits you on the other side.

Reshifting

I had personally witnessed how Patricia had shifted her motivation to follow a strict diet and maintain her optimal motivation. Or, at least, that's what I thought until I asked her to share her story for this book. During the back and forth between us, her story took a U-turn, reminding us of motivation's precarious nature. The six motivational outlooks are represented as bubbles in the Spectrum of Motivation because a different outlook can pop up depending on your reaction—or lack of mindful reaction—to your circumstances.

IN HER OWN WORDS

Patricia: Losing My Way (and Finding It Again and Again!)

When I learned that a decade of suffering might be reversed through diet, I was intrigued. My body's reaction to antibiotics had affected my liver and caused a craving for sweets. My lungs were compromised, affecting my breathing and energy. I learned that I could swap the drugs I'd been prescribed for food as a cure. The new plan resonated with me—especially because it would also help me lose pounds I'd gained from my condition. Then I learned that the diet meant giving up sweets, alcohol, gluten, and dairy. My response? "I could never eat like that! I love my sweets, morning toast, and evening cocktail too much!" Sure, I had dieted in the past to lose a pesky five or ten extra pounds, but I'd never sustained a diet over a long period of time. To make this work, I needed to radically change my eating habits—for life.

Five years later, I'm confident in saying, "I did it." And I am continuing to do it. Not through discipline and willpower but by connecting the diet to a purpose greater than losing weight. Shifting my motivation from "dieting to lose weight" to "eating healthy to get healthy" changed my entire approach to eating. My motivation morphed from an imposed motivational outlook to eliminate foods and drinks I loved to an aligned motivational outlook to heal a chronic illness in the long term. Instead of focusing on the restrictive diet or what I'm giving up, I focus on what I am gaining—a healthy relationship to my body, my self-concept, and

continued

121

my family and friends. By giving up the focus on losing weight, I found that my weight began melting away. My advice to anyone hoping to improve their health or lose weight is to find a higher purpose for eating differently. Recognize that you have a choice with every bite you take to do the right thing for your health. And be aware of how different you feel—keep listening to your body and learning from it.

Thinking we had finally nailed down her story, I sent a draft for her approval. Patricia reviewed her story and wrote me back:

Revisiting this experience in my life has been so good for me! I realize how I need to refresh my aligned motivational outlook. I recently learned that I need to add chocolate and potatoes to my foods-to-avoid list. Not many people can be perfect and avoid all these food groups forever. I certainly can't. Why do you think weight-loss companies are so successful? People fail to sustain the program and gain the weight back. Then they try another "diet." I've managed my pain, but this year my weight spiked, all in my middle. I know that circumstances such as aging and slowing metabolism contribute to the gain, but my optimal motivation is clouded. I still eat healthy most of the time but feel I need to refocus on that other 10 to 15 percent. How do I stop the weight gain and regain my aligned outlook? How do I shift my motivation back to my higher purpose—staying healthy? What suggestions do you have on how to refocus and continue to go down the aligned outlook path? I'll tell you this: just writing down these thoughts is a good start!

Research proves how journaling provides an opportunity for mindfulness, improving mental health and well-being. So it's no surprise that Patricia found value in simply writing emails about her story to remember the reasons for her shift to optimal motivation in the first place. But she also asked important—and common—questions about maintaining optimal motivation that deserve an answer.

For five years, Patricia had consciously linked her eating habits to her value for being healthy and pain free—making the choices that enable her to control her pain. She felt good and wanted to keep manifesting the good feelings. But having achieved her goal of managing her pain, other circumstances intervened that led to a small, but still concerning to her, weight gain. Most of us have the same reaction in this type of situation—we begin reverting to old behaviors or have sub-optimal motivation for adding new behaviors. Losing sight of what's most important and getting caught in the weight-loss trap isn't unusual. Reflecting on the reasons she shifted in the past, Patricia could better understand what was happening in the present.

Maybe you can benefit from the advice I gave Patricia: Practice the skill of motivation by continually reflecting on the reasons for your motivation. Remember your values to maintain your optimal aligned outlook. Your value is for healthy living.

Reflecting on your reasons for shifting can have a more pro-found impact on your future motivation by creating conditions to help you internalize your goal. When your motivation becomes integrated, maintaining your optimal motivation requires less conscious effort. The more mindful you are of your optimal experience, the more likely you are to integrate it over time as a self-identifying activity.

> **Reflecting on your values reminds you that your ideal weight is a by-product, not the object of your motivation.**

Integration means you shift from an aligned outlook statement ("I am a person with a value to eat healthy and keep pain at bay") to an integrated outlook statement ("I am a healthy person"). Eating healthy morphs from something you do to fulfill a value to a way of defining yourself—it's who you are. Integrating eating habits with your self-identity is a powerful tool. But of course, you can use this tool in a variety of situations, as Spiros, a successful entrepreneur in Athens, Greece, reveals in his short story.

IN HIS OWN WORDS Spiros: Know Yourself

I was not happy with my job with an oil company. After a merger, I found myself working in a culture that was alien to me. I had a feeling of not belonging and a lack of choice because priorities were constantly changing with the mood of the business unit leader. The last straw was at a leadership meeting of our business unit, when a colleague said proudly, "We are street fighters!" Suddenly everything made sense—why I felt I didn't belong. I am not a street fighter! In that moment, I decided to leave the company. When I announced it to my boss, I had one of the most liberating feelings I ever had, being myself again, in charge of my career and life!

Spiros nails an important truth. As Polonius says in Shakespeare's *Hamlet*, "To thine own self be true." But that works only if you know thyself! Spiros wasn't judging other street fighters—he was defining himself. He knew street fighting wasn't a self-defining activity and wasn't integrated with his life purpose. The more you know yourself and operate from an integrated outlook, the more likely the decisions you make will not be self-serving but of benefit to the greater good. In this case, I know that Spiros found work more suited to how he defines himself as a compassionate, rational, thoughtful person who believes that collaboration and peacemaking are more effective than street fighting. His story is a reminder that when you choose to act from optimal motivation, you are more likely to make clear and liberating decisions—and less apt to blame lousy circumstances.

You might remember from looking deeper into the optimal outlooks in chapter 6 that one way to attain an integrated outlook is through a significant emotional event that almost instantly forever changes who you are. But the approach shared by Spiros—and the one I recommended to Patricia require time and attention. Reflecting on values-based reasons for your motivation is a potent way to proactively shape the person you want to become.

Discover more about shifting your outlook by visiting the *Master Your Motivation* page at www.susanfowler.com.

10

Beware Fatal Distractions

You are constantly facing distractions from your human potential. Outdated practices in schools, communities, and workplaces—even well-intentioned but ill-advised parenting techniques you experience growing up—can erode your ability to create choice, connection, and competence. But you can avoid many of the most treacherous challenges to your optimal motivation if you are aware of what they are. I call them fatal distractions.

Fatal distractions entice you, lure you in, and cast you into suboptimal motivation day in and day out. If you gravitate toward incentives, bonuses, prizes, rankings, competition, and recognition to feed your motivation, you have surrendered to the distraction of external motivation. If you feel guilty, shameful, or envious of the images portrayed in advertising and social media about the body you should have, the money you could make, or the stuff that would make you happy if only you owned it, you have succumbed to the distraction of imposed motivation. We all fall prey to these distractions without realizing the real price we're paying.

To arm yourself against a fatal distraction, you need to recognize one when you see it. Three of the distractions are so common—and so commonly projected as good things—that you may be surprised at how they erode your choice, connection, and competence without you realizing it. Beware materialism, the search for happiness, and busyness.

SCIENCE SAYS

In their seminal research on motivation, Edward Deci and Richard Ryan report that at our best, we are agentic, meaning we are not merely reactive beings stopped by external forces or driven by inner impulses; we are naturally inclined to learn and extend ourselves, eager to master new skills and apply our talents responsibly. Sometimes we need to be reminded that our human nature is to be "curious, vital, and self-motivated." These characteristics appear "more normative than exceptional."[1]

Yet according to Deci and Ryan, we also know that the human spirit can be diminished or crushed and that individuals sometimes reject growth and responsibility. Too often we see examples of children and adults, regardless of social strata or cultural origin, who are apathetic, alienated, and irresponsible. Quoting from the authors' work directly, "Such non-optimal human functioning can be observed not only in our psychological clinics but also among the millions who, for hours a day, sit passively before their televisions, stare blankly from the back of their classrooms, or wait listlessly for the weekend as they go about their jobs."[2]

I find Deci and Ryan's conclusions poignant. Even the best of us can succumb to the pressures of everyday life and risk slipping into a suboptimal motivational outlook.

Materialism

If you are like most people, you have a complex relationship with money and motivation that deserves attention. Consider the following five statements. Is each true or false?

1. Money cannot buy you happiness.

2. Money will buy things that make you happy.

3. The more money you have, the happier you are.

4. Seeking financial wealth undermines interpersonal relationships.

5. Pursuing money or material wealth results in feeling externally controlled and pressured.

If you've had it drummed into your head since childhood that money doesn't buy you happiness, you probably answered true to statement 1. The old saying makes sense. If money bought happiness, rich people would never suffer from drug abuse, struggle with their weight, agonize over divorce, or find themselves in court defending themselves against sexual harassment, fraud, or other accusations.

Ironically, you may have also answered true to statements 2 and 3. Despite believing that money cannot buy happiness, you might believe that money buys things that make you happy and that the more money you have, the better off you are. But that doesn't make sense. If money doesn't buy you happiness, how can having *more* money buy you happiness? Why would the stuff you buy make you happy?

Research supports a relationship between money and happiness but not in the way you might think. If more money made us happier, we would expect happiness scales to increase as per capita wealth increases. But that isn't the case. Pursuing and achieving material wealth may improve one's short-term mood, but it does not increase one's sustainable happiness.[3] Statements 2 and 3 are simply false.

Now consider your answer to statement 4. If you answered true, you have a partially correct answer. Materialism is a fatal distraction because we fail to acknowledge how it damages the most important determinants of our quality of our life—our values and connection to others.

SCIENCE SAYS

Research indicates that our pursuit of material wealth sabotages our values and relationships, eroding connection. The desire for money and materialism can create pressure that erodes choice. Not having the money or material we desire can erode our sense of competence.[4] Focusing on gaining material wealth crowds out more rewarding pursuits.[5] Recent research reveals a nuance worth understanding. Pursuing financial wealth isn't as important as why you are pursuing it.

Why you focus on money matters, says Jacques Forest, who has written extensively on the motivation behind money.[6] If the motivation behind your pursuit of money is to spend it on others, save time, or gain security, you are more likely to experience well-being than if you spend it on yourself. Money earned for fun (you enjoy doing what earns you money) or with meaning based on values (so you can donate more to charity, for example) results in more optimal functioning than pursuing money for ego or rewards.

Forest emphasizes that only humans give meaning to money. Money is just a means to replace bartering—it is an inanimate object without meaning until we ascribe meaning to it. If your reason for pursuing money is to enhance your image or gain power or status, then your pursuit of money diminishes thriving. However, if you're pursuing money with an aligned, integrated, or inherent motivational outlook, your optimal motivation increases your potential to thrive.

------------------------------■------------------------------

Statement 5—pursuing money or material wealth results in feeling controlled and pressured—is true. The pursuit of money or wealth is a low-quality goal fueled by junk food motivation that erodes choice, connection, and competence. The lack of control along with added pressure is a disaster if your goal requires creativity, discretionary effort, or sustained high productivity and performance.

Maybe you've heard about the "contract year phenomenon" in sports. Empirical studies demonstrate that Major League Baseball and National Basketball Association players can summon peak performance and great stats during the season their contracts are up for renewal.[7] The promise of big-money contracts energizes them—but proves more helpful to their personal stats than to the team. After signing their dream deal, they are unable to sustain their level of performance, experiencing a two-year postcontract performance crash that drops them below their one-year precontract baseline.

Money is one of the most sinister fatal distractions because we all need money (or its equivalent) to survive. But there is a difference between needing money and being motivated by money. When money is your driving force, you do not control it; you are controlled by it—robbing you of choice. Money distracts you from high-quality reasons to do what you do—undermining connection. Money becomes the end goal instead of learning and growth—diminishing opportunities for competence.

A young sales rep admitted that she was money motivated. I encouraged her to find a high-quality, values-based reason for making her numbers instead of focusing on the incentive she was being offered for selling a new product. Months later, she confessed that she'd discounted my advice. She explained that the $2,000 incentive was enticing to her as a single mother with limited resources. She felt she *should* strive to win the bonus—she'd have felt guilty if she didn't go for it knowing the bills she had to pay. But then she shared how those feelings gave way to more guilt as she found herself "pushing" the product for the wrong reasons and risking her clients' trust. Her excitement at having a new product in her quiver of client solutions was overshadowed by the pressure of getting the incentive, which affected her overall performance. The fatal distraction of work based on incentives proved too toxic—she's no longer with the organization.

And here is a great sadness. Operating from materialistic values not only undermines your well-being but also negatively affects the health and well-being of others. When your focus is on material pursuits, you become less compassionate and empathetic. Your values shape the way you work, play, live, and make decisions. And those decisions impact the world around you.[8]

Money does not buy happiness or the things that make you happy. In fact, the more materialistic your core values are, the more the quality of your life is diminished. A lower quality of life is reflected in a variety of ways, including low energy, anxiety, substance abuse, negative emotions, depression, and a likelihood to engage in high-risk behaviors.[9]

With the insight gained through recent motivation research and the fascinating field of social neuroscience showing how our need to connect with others is more basic than our need for food and shelter,[10] you can master your motivation and shift your focus from fatal distractions such as money and materialism to the more empowering values of acceptance, compassion, emotional intimacy, caring for the welfare of others, and contributing to the world around you. Denying fatal distractions will not only improve the quality of your life but also create a ripple effect that ultimately improves the quality of life for others, for the reality is that the most important things in life cannot be bought for any amount of money. Indeed, they are priceless.

The Search for Happiness

Neuroscientists love to point out that status or power lights up the same part of the brain that lights up when you are happy. Consider what the word *happiness* really signifies. It derives from *hap* (n.) meaning "chance, fortune." *Happy* means "'lucky, favored by fortune, . . . prosperous;' of events, 'turning out well.'"[11] Happiness depends on what happens. By its nature, something "making you happy" is antithetical to your psychological need for choice—the perception that you are the source of your own actions. If you are happy for the wrong reasons, such as winning at the cost of someone else's losing—you undermine connection. Being senselessly happy can be wonderful, but if you never learn from your happiness, over time you risk competence.

Instead of searching for happiness, an option is to focus on mastering your motivation, as Stephanie, a senior contracts manager in the aerospace industry, describes in her story.

IN HER OWN WORDS

Stephanie: From Happiness to Optimal Motivation

I was devastated by the announcement. A business integration project meant the closure of the local site where I'd worked for twenty-nine years. As a senior member of the management team, I was expected to support the goal of transitioning two hundred employees who had dedicated twenty-five plus years of service and close the site within two years.

I simply could not see value in combining the business with the other divisions. I felt great disappointment that the decision was announced without input from the local experts. It felt like a failed plan from the start—and a total waste of energy. Keeping up with the daily responsibilities of managing my team and serving our customers was already a challenge; the thought of developing and implementing a detailed plan to transfer the requisite knowledge and skills to two divisions across the country added to the sense of overwhelm. I bounced back and forth between a disinterested motivational outlook, where I just wanted to put my head in the sand until it was all over, and an imposed motivational outlook, feeling the pressure, frustration, and anger over the whole situation.

Shortly after the announcement, I made a values choice. I shifted to an aligned motivational outlook to serve people by encouraging them to hold their heads high throughout this difficult process. To that end, a coworker and I decided to capture the proud story of the business as a tribute to its fantastic people

continued

and products. A team was formed, and after two years of hard work in addition to our full-time jobs, a book documenting the history of the people and the products was published and distributed at an all-employee event. The final chapter was a tribute to the employees as a reminder that the success of the business was a direct result of its uniquely talented, dedicated, and loyal employees. Due to the overwhelming positive response, the company chose to make this standard work for all future plant closures.

I consciously made another shift to an aligned motivational outlook—I made a deliberate choice to do the right thing with my team despite my difficulty with the decision to close the business. This enabled me to demonstrate my values of integrity, loyalty, and service. I announced my commitment to stick it out to the end of my team's two-year journey and steward each of them to new opportunities. This was particularly challenging for me given my distrust of senior management and my desire for stability. However, the action paid off by building trust and commitment within my team, resulting in zero attrition within the department compared to an average of 30 percent across the division. Two members received promotions to managers at the new sites, and each of the rest of the employees received offers for new and exciting positions, while I chose to obtain a master's degree.

Mastering my motivation gave me the courage to rise above my need for happiness in the moment, take on the difficult challenge of publishing a book, and demonstrate values important to me—to inspire others to master their own motivation and seize new opportunities.

Stephanie's proactive approach to focusing on the quality of her motivation at work resulted in something far richer than fleeting happiness. She created a lasting legacy.

Busyness

If work is your life, then how do you disconnect? If you are challenged to let go even when you aren't at work, perhaps it's time to explore why. The reasons for not disconnecting matter. How do you create connection outside of work if you never disconnect from work?

Maybe you wear busyness as a badge of honor: "I'm so busy doing important things that I don't have time for anything else!" If that sounds familiar, you might consider how it is that many of the most successful people in the world find time to refresh their spirit and connect with people they love? You have the same twenty-four hours a day as everyone else on the planet.

What fuels your inability to disconnect from work is important to understand. Consider the differences between these two reasons for not being able to disconnect:

- I need to stay connected to reap the rewards of my busyness: power and control, money and adult toys, and social status.

- I work multiple jobs, day in and day out, for higher-level values such as providing an education for my children, supporting those less fortunate, and meeting my obligations with gratitude and without fanfare.

People have told me they don't want to disconnect because they are so passionate about their work. Fair enough. But if your passion is fueled by fatal distractions—power, status, image, money—your passion may prove obsessive, not harmonious. You don't control obsessive passion—it controls you.[12] If you have obsessive passion, your inability to disconnect is more an addiction than a choice. If you are caught up in busyness for the wrong reasons, your busyness is a fatal distraction that erodes choice, connection, and competence.

A young Google executive famous for her round-the-clock work ethic and success at developing a program most of us know by name opted into a coaching initiative to help her manage her time. On our second call, she revealed that she requested coaching for her personal life, not her professional life. Her health was at risk, she worried that she wasn't spending quality time with her children, and she suspected her husband was having an affair. I had coached other Google execs and not gotten this deep into personal issues. I am not, after all, a licensed psychologist. I explained that we could focus on her work practices and monitor how they affected her personal issues.

A month into the coaching, she announced that she'd scheduled a vacation—a true sign of progress. But she expressed concern. What if she couldn't disconnect and be fully present with her family? We had practiced the skill of motivation during our sessions, including reflecting through mindfulness. But she said she needed five specific actions to help her disconnect. In the spirit of dampening her need to overachieve, I agreed on three: change what you listen for, ask why, and notice your energy.

Change What You Listen For

Whether at work or home, you often listen with an ulterior motive. You listen for information you can use to get an intended result. You listen for clues you can act on, a point you can elaborate on, or a gap in logic you can fill.

To disconnect from busyness and create connection, change what you listen for. Listen for someone's needs—not so you can act on them but as an act of kindness and compassion. Listen for the essence of what the person is saying—not the content, but the emotions.

Don't hold yourself accountable for acting on what you hear. Simply change what you listen for and be with the person and his or her needs—not your need to do something, say something, or make something happen.

Ask Why

Before scheduling an activity, giving someone feedback, or taking an action, stop and ask yourself the following questions:

- Why am I doing this?
- Why do I need to do this?
- Why should I do this?
- Why would I do this?

If you cannot answer the questions with a meaningful value, noble purpose, or inherent joy, don't take the action. If reducing tension and stress is desirable, consider the source of the tension and stress. If you are following meaningful values, a noble purpose, and your bliss, you probably aren't feeling stressed!

When you are living an authentic life, your actions are meaningful. You work hard, but your work is focused. Your work is important but not an indicator of your worth. It presents challenges but doesn't leave you physically weak or wishing you had time to paint, do yoga, or spend quality time with your family.

Notice Your Energy

Are you radiating positive energy that reflects mindfulness, lack of judgment, and an openness to what is? Do you generate positive energy in others or drain it? Does your energy impart tension, stress, and busyness or promote love, compassion, and healing? The world is energy. You can channel it and purify it or use it and pollute it. Notice the energy you project, but don't judge it. Just reflect: "That's interesting."

My client returned from her vacation with a newfound ability to appreciate the moment—and the people sharing that moment. As witness to her revelations, I became more convinced than ever that mindfulness is essential for mastering your motivation. Most of our suboptimal motivation—and the world's suffering—is born from our inability to disconnect from the fatal distractions that lure us into busyness and unhealthy patterns of behavior: our fears, distorted stories that we think are true, implicit or explicit bias, prejudice, and preconceived notions that obscure an innate connection to our authentic self and the greater good.

Studies on mindfulness show that with minimal effort, we are more empathetic and compassionate—not just to others but to ourselves. Imagine if we all became mindfully aware that what we do to others, we do to ourselves—and vice versa. So this weekend, mindfully change what you listen for, ask why before acting, and notice your energy. Take a break from the fatal distraction of busyness and appreciate the true fruits of your labor.

For more insight on fatal distractions, visit the *Master Your Motivation* page at www.susanfowler.com.

11

.

Work Hazards

Traditional techniques for motivating people at work have proven ineffective, faulty, or downright wrong.[1] Yet well-intentioned managers still drive for results, promote suboptimal motivation, and make creating choice, connection, and competence at work a real challenge. A question worth asking is Why?

I got a glimpse into the answer when a vice president of sales cornered me during a break at a sales meeting. "I'm about to be embarrassed," he told me. I looked at him quizzically. He continued, "I'm about to announce the incentive plans for selling our new product. I didn't realize you'd be here. I know how you feel about incentives."

I nodded in agreement. I am an outspoken advocate for the body of evidence proving how external rewards are a notorious form of suboptimal motivation with a detrimental effect on performance. Our conversation proceeded something like this:

ME: Why are you offering incentives?

VP, *with a tone of "Isn't it obvious?"*: To increase sales.

ME: Are you assuming the sales reps won't sell the product without an incentive? Is the product flawed? Do your customers not really need it?

VP: No, the product is good and our customers want it. But our sales reps get in the habit of selling what they have, not the new stuff, so we need to incentivize them to sell something new.

If the vice president's answer had been "Yes, the product is flawed and our customers don't want it," we would have had an entirely different conversation about using incentives as a disguise to bribe people into potentially immoral and unethical behavior.

ME: Why would sales reps not take advantage of a new product? Have they not had enough exposure to the product to advocate for it? Are they lazy? Are they bored? Are they so content that they don't need to generate more sales? Are they so conditioned with incentives that they don't care about customer needs? Are they not aware of the benefits the new product offers clients?

VP, *with a tone of resignation*: I don't know! It's just what we always do when we release a new product!

We made a quick change in plans. After the break, I introduced the vice president, explaining that he was about to announce an incentive plan for the new product launch. My intent was to promote choice, connection, and competence to counter the inevitable pressure that winning incentives generates.

I encouraged the sales reps to internalize the incentives not as their reason to sell, but as the company's way of communicating a priority. I asked the reps to consider why the company developed the product in the first place. I asked them to think deeply about their own reasons for selling the product and how that aligned with their values for selling.

Would the new product improve people's lives in a meaning-ful way, lead to a deeper client relationship, or help clients solve an important problem?

Sure, I would have preferred that they abandon incentives altogether. But encouraging the reps to look beyond the incentives to their own reasons for selling was a fair start at promoting choice, connection, and competence. At the next break, I found the sales reps' feedback heartening. They thanked me for my comments, sharing that they had a fresh perspective they thought would prove helpful not only to their sales but to their customers. One seasoned rep told me he felt like a monkey doing tricks for coins when incentives got dangled but could now reframe that picture more pos-itively. Several reps confessed that they'd gladly accept the incentives but were frankly insulted by the implication that they couldn't see the value of selling the new product without an incentive.

What if the sales managers had taken the time to facili-tate conversations so the reps could have discovered their own positive reasons for selling the product? Instead, the managers defaulted to tried and *not true* carrot-and-stick motivation.

But don't cast all the blame on your manager for resort-ing to carrots or sticks, praise or pressure, and promises or threats. Have you ever seen the competencies your manager is being held accountable for achieving? *Drive for results, exceed goals successfully, constantly and consistently be one of the top performers, be very bottom-line oriented, steadfastly push self and others for results, assess staff members' hot buttons and use them to get the best out of the staff*—these are real expectations from real performance plans.

Organizations, leaders, teachers, and parents don't bamboo-zle you with external or imposed motivation with the inten-tion of undermining choice, connection, and competence, but

I am saddened by how many of them seem fearful of exploring alternative approaches to motivation. Much of my consulting is teaching managers and executives how to nurture rather than sabotage people's choice, connection, and competence. But traditional beliefs about rewards, incentives, recognition and praise, power, status, and image die hard.

If your organization and manager see the light when it comes to the truth of human motivation, consider yourself lucky. But the real job falls to you to move beyond the carrots and sticks that can beat you up.

Working for the wrong reasons diminishes results. Working to create choice, connection, and competence yields results beyond expectations.

Since motivation is at the heart of everything you do or don't do, why depend on others to do what you can do for yourself? You will discover that proactively creating choice, connection, and competence at work is worth the effort. Three ways to begin are to flip feedback, deepen connection, and advocate for justice.

Flip the Feedback

Getting pure feedback on your performance is essential to your development and ultimate success at anything you do in life. But you face a big problem when it comes to feedback. Recent studies reveal that in the workplace, most managers don't like giving feedback—especially when it's critical or reinforcing direction already given. Worse, when managers do give feedback, they aren't good at it—despite the money, time, and effort that's gone into training them to deliver effective feedback. In fact, 64 percent of the time, their feedback has been shown to do more harm than good.[2] If this is true at work, imagine how challenging it is to get effective feedback from spouses and partners, friends, parents—or even athletic and artistic coaches.

Why continue to depend on others to give you the feedback you need to develop and grow? Maybe it's time you flipped the feedback. Don't wait for it; ask for it. Neuroscience provides additional evidence for flipping the feedback paradigm. Asking for feedback sets up a more responsive brain condition. Requesting feedback delivers the information you need when you need it but also results in less defensiveness—meaning you are more likely to hear what you need to hear and act on it.[3]

Years ago, I called a group of subject-matter experts together to discuss a project I was developing. I was so excited to gain insight from their combined experience and knowledge—especially since learning is one of my top values. I described the project, my hopes and dreams, and my opinions on several provocative ideas. To my dismay, I got no response. People just sat there staring at me blankly. I called a break—but not before making some inane comment like "Who were you before you died?"

During the break, Kathy, one of the participants, pulled me aside and whispered, "Susan, I think you called us here for a dialogue and you seem disappointed that people aren't speaking up. If that's true, would you be open to some feedback that might be helpful?" I shook my head yes, eager to hear what she had to say. Without hesitation Kathy explained, "Your style is so exuberant and direct that I think people figure you already have all the answers. I think you shut them down. That's how *I* feel—you brought us here to listen but not participate."

I was stunned. I told Kathy that shutting her down was the opposite of my intention. I was open-minded and hungry for collaboration. "Then," she said compassionately, "you might want to adjust your style."

I not only adjusted my style in the meeting but began observing myself, working to improve my approach to leading meetings and teams. To this day, I am grateful for the courage it took Kathy to provide me that crucial feedback. I also realize that many people—even people who love me and managers who depend on my performance—don't have the courage, inclination, or skill to deliver that kind of feedback. That's why I honed the skill of flipping the feedback.

If you're interested in developing this skill, do the following exercise. Tomorrow morning, try a bold start to your day. Flip the feedback and ask your manager, coworkers, or staff members, "What feedback can you give me that you think could help me do [fill-in-the-blank] better?"

Perhaps you will find, as I did, that flipping the feedback is a powerful skill for creating the choice, connection, and competence required for generating optimal motivation. When you recognize the difference between what you are doing and what you could do, you can choose what steps to take next—creating choice. When you give your manager or others an opening to share their observations, insights, and ideas to help you develop, you demonstrate that you care about what they think and provide them the chance to express that they care about you too—creating connection. When you receive information that is relevant and timely, you learn from the feedback—creating competence.

If you want to take flipping the feedback to the next level, then when you learn something of value from the feedback you receive, *act on it*. Put what you've learned to use. Asking for feedback and then acting on it demonstrates that you have the willingness to learn and the courage to face the truth.[4]

Deepen Connection

Your greatest opportunity to master your motivation at work is in creating connection. Even if you create choice and competence, they are incomplete without the meaning, sense of purpose, or fulfillment of connection.

You create connection when you find meaning in whatever you are doing—especially at work.

Missy is an administrative assistant for an energy company in Wyoming who took creating connection to heart. Part of Missy's job was to triage calls coming in from the field. One lineman called in regularly and Missy would forward each call to the appropriate person. After months of enduring the lineman's grievances and rants, no one would take his calls. After attending a training session on the skill of mastering your motivation, Missy thought about the lineman's psychological needs. She realized that his job gave him plenty of choice—he had full autonomy on how to deal with situations in his territory. As one of the most seasoned veterans in the company, it would be unusual for him not to appreciate his competence. But his job meant being alone in the Wyoming wilderness, far from headquarters and without regular contact with coworkers. Missy concluded that the lineman's weekly complaints were really a cry for connection.

The next time the lineman called in, Missy took the call herself and engaged him in a conversation. Now he calls in weekly just to chat with Missy for a few minutes. The complaints stopped; a friendship blossomed. Missy's company was so pleased with what happened that it sponsored her attendance at a conference where I was speaking so she could share the story with me.

I was impressed with Missy's awareness that helped her identify the lineman's lack of connection. I was also struck by how she created her own choice by accepting responsibility to deal with the lineman, created connection by developing a genuine bond with him and giving meaning to an otherwise menial task of answering phones, and created competence by gaining the skills to deal effectively with conflict. By proactively helping someone else master his motivation, she had mastered her own.

Advocate for Justice

If you work for an organization that you think is unfair, you have a choice. You can leave. You can continue feeling disconnected and joyless but not leave (or as it's often described, you can quit and stay—rationalizing that you need the money). Or you can choose to stay and stand up for justice. You can work to open closed-door policies where information is used as a form of control. You can campaign against wage discrimination, favoritism, and implicit bias. It is possible to petition for equal wages without being motivated by money. You can promote fair goals without being motivated by a free ride. You can encourage unbiased treatment without being motivated by self-serving interests. You can request a seat at the table without being motivated by status or power.

When you advocate for the principles of justice and fairness, you create deeper connection for yourself and with others.

Connection is eroded when you experience unfairness.
You create connection when you advocate for justice.

Unfortunately, too many people wallow in circumstances that kill their spirit and rob their souls. A recent bank scandal is a sad example of what happens when company practices erode connection and employees fail to create it for themselves.[5] Executives set unrealistic goals, creating a situation where salespeople ended up cheating over eighty-five thousand customers to achieve their goals. In the aftermath of the fraud, over five thousand employees were fired and over $110 million paid in fines, with the possibility pending of an additional billion-dollar fine.[6] The world was stunned at the audacity of the deceit. As a customer, I was angry. As an advocate of optimal motivation, I was heartbroken.

But bad bosses weren't the only ones who perpetrated fraud. Every employee who succumbed to the dishonest schemes shares the blame. Perhaps even sadder is that individual employees didn't stand up and say, "I won't do this." Regretfully, individuals never linked their goals to their own values or a noble purpose. Nothing was stopping employees from doing the right thing. But they caved in to greed and fear.

Tragically, we have too many examples of organizations filled with employees who work with suboptimal motivation doing the wrong things for the wrong reasons. Don't be one of those people. Be aware of your choices—and how the decisions you make align (or don't) to values you claim are important to you. Recognize that

- A work ethic without ethics leads to corruption

- A goal without a mission takes you nowhere important

- A life without work based on values has little value

- *Empowerment* without a sense of power is an empty word

- Empowerment is not something that is done to you; it is something you do for yourself

Think about this: 75 percent of the time you are awake is spent getting to and from work, working, or thinking about work. When it comes to your motivation, there is no such thing as compensatory need satisfaction. If you are not creating choice, connection, and competence at work, you are probably too tired or busy to create enough to compensate outside of work. That doesn't mean you shouldn't focus on creating choice, connection, and competence outside of work—just that you need to be sure you create it at work too. That is exactly what Rocio did working in the Mexico City office of a global company.

IN HER OWN WORDS **Rocio: Shifting My Focus**

I was new to the company—less than a year in—when I had my first performance review. I had delivered more training sessions than anyone in the history of the company, I had great comments from my internal and external clients, and yet my boss didn't congratulate me at all. Just the opposite: he gave me a very low review. I felt terrible, unappreciated, and even bullied by the way he gave me the feedback. I felt so bad, I began working just so my boss would see the value in me. I caught myself working for his attention and praise—motivated by an external motivational outlook. It was exhausting!

So after learning the skill of motivation, I decided to shift my focus. I started being mindful of why I was doing my work and how I wanted to feel about it. I decided I wanted to work and feel good without external recognition. I started to see the purpose behind the training sessions I was doing (I was helping others learn and understand things more easily), and I felt good about it! I decided any time I started to feel I needed external motivation, I was going to self-regulate by remembering how good I feel when I am mindful of the purpose behind my work.

After I made this decision, I started to enjoy my work and stopped needing or expecting external motivation. This took off so much pressure; I got faster in my deliveries, and people even told me I was smiling more!

Ironically, a few months after my shift in motivation, my boss started to recognize my work—even publicly. I appreciated it, but I didn't need it.

Rocio discovered what studies show: When you proactively create choice, connection, and competence, you are more likely to experience sustained high performance and reduced strain and fatigue—and have the wherewithal to devote quality time to health, family and friends, and all those dreams you'd pursue, inside and outside work, if you only had the energy![7]

Learn more about motivation at work, by visiting the *Master Your Motivation* page at www.susanfowler.com.

12.

Can People Change?

If you have a choice—and you do—why wouldn't you choose an optimal outlook? If you apply the skill of motivation, you can be optimally motivated whenever and wherever you choose. So why not always choose to create choice, connection, and competence?

The excuse I usually get is if you don't have an inherent outlook for a goal or situation, shifting your motivation requires conscious effort. Shifting your motivation becomes just one more thing to add to an already full to-do list.

I counter this argument with great science proving how optimal motivation improves everything from productivity and performance to creativity and innovation to mental and physical well-being. Despite my compelling arguments, some people remain unconvinced—they claim to be fine eating hamburger. Why spend the extra effort to eat steak at every meal? Save your shifting efforts for special occasions.

One day, I found myself not practicing what I preach. I realized that I will never have an inherent motivational outlook going through security at an airport. The experience is designed not to be fun or enjoyable but serious and challenging. I found myself asking the question I'd often asked others: Is shifting my motivation for something I don't inherently enjoy, and never will, worth the time and effort?

Mastering My Own Motivation

I was in a hurry, as usual. Not because I was late. I was just in a hurry—it's my nature. I arrived at the airport feeling pressured to get through security in the shortest amount of time possible. I evaluated each line to find the shortest and fastest. I follow self-imposed guidelines: Don't get in a line with a family, especially with small kids. Don't get in a line with a lot of men. (Sorry, men, this is not a sexist comment but an observation confirmed by people who notice such things. Most of you don't carry purses, so you take time emptying your pockets. You carefully remove your jacket and fold it neatly before laying it in the bin, whereas most women just throw their sweaters or jackets in the bin.) And finally, find an agent who doesn't appear obsessed with every little detail.

That morning, for some reason, I caught myself. I noticed how stressed I was. I was ashamed. I teach this stuff, but there I was gritting my teeth, clenching my fists, and about to lurch into a line I'd determined was the shortest and fastest. "Hmm. Maybe this is a good time to walk my talk and practice the skill of motivation," I thought. But even as I entered the practice, I wondered if it was worth the effort—I'd always have to go through security and I'd always hate it, right? Still, I proceeded.

First Action: Identify My Outlook

Identifying my outlook was easy. I had an imposed motivational outlook. I knew it wasn't the disinterested motivational outlook because I was feeling too much angst, pressure, resentment—and shame (for feeling all those negative emotions!).

Second Action: Shift My Outlook

I had no choice—I had to go through security to get to my flight. I didn't have connection—I don't find personal

151

meaning in going through security, nor do I think it's all that effective at stopping terrorists who don't want to be stopped. But I had competence—I'm an expert at getting through security efficiently.

I asked myself the questions to create choice, connection, and competence. I didn't get far with the choice questions. Yes, I chose to accept work that requires me to fly. And if I fly, I accept that I need to go through security. The logic was there, but an emotional shift eluded me. I still didn't like or want to go through security.

The questions to awaken connection held more promise. Could going through security align with one of my values: compassion, curiosity, learning? Learning! What could I learn by going through security? It hit me in an instant: patience; I could learn patience. I asked, Why is patience important to me? My body resonated with something I'd longed for—a sense of peace. I admire people who exude a centered calmness. I've always had an exuberant energy that bounces off walls. Some people find it engaging, but I'm sure many find it aggravating and exhausting.

I asked myself, How do I practice patience? The answer was obvious: get in the longest line. I found a doozy: a long line with a family. Not just any family but a young couple with a toddler, a newborn, and all the paraphernalia. (I didn't know you could take that much stuff through security.) I got in line behind them, and the father asked me if I wanted to go ahead of them. He could tell I was efficient and would be through before they even began putting their stuff on the belt. I smiled weakly and told him, "No, thank you." I whispered to myself, "I'm practicing patience."

Watching the young couple struggle with all their stuff was painful. Boldly I offered, "Would it help if I hold your baby?" They didn't hesitate. Suddenly, I was holding a precious baby. They finished loading up the belt and were about to head through the scanner when I reminded them, "Don't you want your baby back?" On the other side, I again held the baby as they packed up before we all went our separate ways.

Waiting at the gate for my flight to board, I noticed the young father approaching me. "I'm glad I found you," he said. "My wife and I are so embarrassed. This is the first time we've ever traveled with two kids. We had no idea how hard it would be! We couldn't have gotten through security without you, but we never even thanked you. So we just want you to know how grateful we are. Your help really made a difference to us." Flustered, I said, "No, no, thank you! Holding your baby was my pleasure!" We continued thanking each until my plane started boarding.

Third Action: Reflect on My Outlook

Sitting in my seat on the plane, I reflected on what had just happened. I had successfully shifted from suboptimal to optimal motivation. By practicing patience, I experienced an aligned motivational outlook—self-regulating and letting go of my typical anxiety felt good. I took a mental note to remember that feeling. Then I realized I'd also experienced the inherent motivational outlook—holding that baby was fun. I love babies. But my next reflection revealed a radical shift that rocked my world. The father told me I'd made a difference to them. My life purpose is to use my speaking and writing opportunities to be a catalyst for good. I had just fulfilled my purpose by helping a family go through security. I could be a catalyst for good dozens of times a year just going through security!

Years later, I still proactively create choice and connection—I choose to go through security so I can practice patience, express compassion, continue learning, and be a catalyst for good. I still create competence, but now my efficiency is used to help an elderly man who's confused by what he's supposed to remove or leave on, show kindness to security agents who hear people's complaints day in and day out, and of course, hold babies whenever it seems helpful and appropriate. I am reminded that fulfilling my life purpose may be helpful to others, but it also creates choice, connection, and competence—yielding more gifts to me than I give to others.

Mastering my motivation to go through security did more than make an annoying necessity tolerable. My entire experience was elevated—creating a ripple effect beyond the security gate. I proved to myself that shifting even the most benign routine from suboptimal to optimal motivation can yield a major change that's worth the effort.

My story leads to a fundamental question at the heart of this book. Can people change? Can you change? Before you answer, consider how change happens and the role your motivation plays.

How Does Change Happen?

If you believe that your personality is hardwired, mostly a matter of genetics, and simply who you are—that you can't change your basic nature—then you won't care about how change happens. But if you sense that your human nature is complex yet capable of growth, then you might be curious about how change happens.

When you are challenged with impending change, you may lapse into the disinterested outlook, stick your head in the sand, and hope it passes. But when your organization adopts the hot-desking trend (shared workspaces) or a new enterprise-wide platform or your society moves from the agricultural to industrial to information age, you will eventually have to pull your head from the sand and face a new reality.

Instead of feeling left behind, you can take advantage of the transition using the science of motivation and what we know about the way people experience change.[1]

> **Everyone goes through predictable stages of concern during a change.**

Early in the change process, you have both information concerns and personal concerns—you need to know what the change is, why it's happening, and how it will affect you. Don't make the mistake of avoiding your personal concerns until you get all the detailed information about the change. You can sense when change is coming: word leaks out, rumors and half-truths are spread, and you find yourself making up your own story without the benefit of knowledge. If you smell the smoke of change, you are already fearing the fire. You are likely to fall into suboptimal motivation—immediately sticking your head in the sand, going along with the change in the hope of gaining some reward, or feeling anxious and imposed on.

Enter the skill of motivation. To address your personal concerns about the change you are experiencing, adapt the questions to create choice, connection, and competence:

1. Choice: What choices do I have? People tend to forget they have choices when faced with a change made without their input or consent. But remember, you always have choices. You can choose to come to work or not; to give your all or bide your time working in fear and expecting the worst; to learn, grow, and contribute or hold back out of resentment and retaliation.

   When you realize you have choices, you are less likely to see change and a potential lack of security as threatening.

2. Connection: What meaning can I make from all of this? In times of turmoil, you need to attribute meaning to the madness around you. Consider taking a proactive approach to help identify opportunities to serve others, deepen relationships, and contribute to the greater good. Connect your work to a higher purpose. Instead of simply driving for results, challenge yourself to examine higher-quality reasons for why results are important.

3. Competence: What can I learn? Never forget that your nature is to learn and grow every day. However, without a conscious effort, you won't tend to notice what you are learning—or even that you are learning at all. Asking yourself what you stand to learn from a change prompts your awareness of your innate desire for continued growth—and how important it is to your sense of well-being. A change can help rekindle your innate enthusiasm for learning.

Change happens. Don't shield yourself from what's happening or obfuscate the truth in hopes of protecting yourself. Motivation is a key factor in developing resilience. When you master your motivation despite the chaos or conditions, you can satisfy your psychological needs and experience optimal motivation. You can thrive in the midst of change, uncertainty, and ambiguity. But managing or surviving change is different than changing yourself. Can people change? Can *you* change?

Can You Change?

A zebra never changes his stripes. A leopard can't change her spots. People don't change; they just reveal their real selves over time. Are these statements common wisdom or gross misunderstandings of human nature?

What about the frog and the scorpion? A popular story told to explain that people don't change their basic nature begins with the scorpion asking the frog for a ride across the river. The frog responds, "Are you kidding? Of course not! I know you, scorpion, and you would sting me and I'd die. No way will I carry you on my back!" The scorpion challenges the frog, "Why would I do that? If I sting you and you die, we both drown. You have nothing to fear by carrying me across the river." The frog decides that what the scorpion said makes sense, so he agrees to the request.

Midway across the river, the scorpion stings the frog. As the frog gasps his last breath before drowning, he implores the scorpion, "Why? Why did you sting me, knowing we will both drown?" The scorpion replies, "It's my nature."

Is it helpful to relate our human nature to zebras, leopards, scorpions, and frogs, belying the idea that people are self-determinant beings capable of change?

Sure, examples of people who don't change are plentiful. Despite backlash and personal repercussions, a convicted felon continues his illegal lifestyle at the risk of breaking parole and being sent back to prison. A drama queen continually pushes people from her life, despite her need for meaningful relationships. Leaders do what's comfortable for them in the moment rather than what's best for those they lead.

Because evidence of people not changing is abundant— and because we may have struggled or failed in our own attempts to change—we tend to assume people can't change: Instead, we need to contemplate this question: *Could* the felon, the drama queen, or self-absorbed leaders change? Is change possible?

The evidence points to yes. You are constantly changing— physically, mentally, emotionally, and spiritually. Medical research reveals that the cells in your body are in a continual cycle of death and renewal. Brain studies show that extraordinary neuroplasticity enables you to change neural pathways and, thus, habits and behaviors. Mindfulness research poses exciting possibilities for developing empathy, making better decisions, and experiencing enhanced emotional regulation. Motivation science points to how fulfilling your need for choice, connection, and competence affects almost everything you do and feel.

A common thread of every great spiritual practice throughout history is the belief that human beings can raise their conscious awareness and live life at a higher level. The belief that change is possible entices you to greet a new day. Hope is a belief that things—and you—can change for the better.

Not believing that you can and do change is to wonder what your human experience is about. We are not scorpions or frogs. We are beings with self-determination and the ability to reflect and mindfully choose who we are, what we believe, and how we behave. The skill to master your motivation may be your greatest opportunity to evolve, grow in wisdom, and be the light the world so desperately needs.

Learn more about motivation and change by visiting the *Master Your Motivation* page at www.susanfowler.com.

AFTERWORD

Ken Blanchard

When Susan Fowler asked me if I would write the afterword to this book, I was thrilled because I'm a great admirer of hers. Susan is one of the greatest learners I know—always pushing herself, and all of us, to think about things differently. In *Master Your Motivation*, Susan asks you, her reader, to think about your development in a whole new way.

This book is not about *managers working with you*—a subject I've written about for years. Instead, it is about *you working with yourself*. Bringing these two concepts together has been an interesting outgrowth of many conversations I've had with Susan. Let me explain.

People sometimes ask me, if somebody took everything away from me that I've taught over the last forty years except one thing, what would I want to hold on to? My answer has always been the Second Secret of the One Minute Manager— One Minute Praisings. They are all about accentuating the positive and catching people doing things right. When I started to talk with Susan about her work, she explained to me that while she thinks my answer is well-intentioned and that it's great to notice the good work people are doing, she sees a problem.

You see, the second part of a One Minute Praising is for your manager to tell you how your actions made her feel and to encourage you to keep up the good work. Susan's concern is that when your manager says how your good performance makes *her* feel, the focus of the praising conversation turns away from you (the praisee) and back to your manager (the praiser). I think Susan makes a good point. She suggests an alternative scenario.

Let's say you're the manager. What if, instead of telling a person how you feel about his effort or performance, you were to ask him how his good work made *him* feel? What if you kept the ball in the other person's court? It might go something like this:

"Hey Jeremy, I just heard that your conversion rates went up 15 percent this quarter—5 percent over your goal. That must have taken a lot of work on your part. How do you feel about your effort?"

"I'm really happy about it. It *was* hard work, but it paid off. Thanks for asking!"

Susan and I both want to help people move from dependence on others to independence—and the sooner that process starts, the better. When your manager gives you feedback in a way that leaves you thinking about *your own* actions, rather than *her opinion* of your actions, the responsibility falls to you to evaluate your own effort and performance.

I'm excited about the idea of you evaluating your own work and coming to your own conclusions. *After* you have a sense of how well you're doing, you can ask other people for input. Susan calls this "flipping the feedback." What have they noticed about your performance? In this case, *you* are taking the initiative to get feedback—not waiting around for others to tell you whether they think you're good or not. What would you say to them? If you were to ask your manager, you could say, "I've been doing this particular job for a while and it seems I've met the expectations you and I discussed—but getting feedback about what *you* think would be helpful." Flip the feedback—*ask* for it rather than *waiting* for it. Go ahead and ask for feedback from your coworkers too.

Remember, the earlier in life you start moving toward accepting responsibility and taking initiative to get better at what you do, the better and quicker you're going to move from dependence to independence. I think some people get stuck where they are—they start relying on other people's praise, recognition, and redirection, not their own. And they also get stuck on what they think about when they consider their self-worth.

My friend Bob Buford wrote an interesting book called *Halftime*, where he said that sometime in midlife, people find themselves in the locker room thinking about coming out for the second half of their life. Most people want to move from success to significance—to make a shift from getting to giving, in a big-picture way. But Susan says, Why wait until midlife for that transition? Why not start looking at where you are in your life's journey right now?

When your self-worth is based on external success factors, your focus tends to be on how much money you make, the recognition you get for your efforts, and the power and status you gain. That becomes the scorecard. Now, there's nothing wrong with making good money, being recognized for your efforts, or gaining power and status—but if that's who you think you are, the only way to maintain your self-worth is to get more of those things. That's why some people are all about attaining a more powerful position, more money, and more recognition.

So what is *significance*?

The opposite of accumulation of wealth is *generosity* of your time, talent, treasure, and touch (support and encouragement). The opposite of recognition is *service*. The opposite of power and status is *loving relationships*.

If you focus on success in terms of external rewards and the opinion of others to define who you are and your self-worth, you'll never get to significance. But in my experience, if you focus on generosity, service, and loving relationships, you'll achieve the feeling of purpose, contentment, and joy that comes with living a life of significance. My mother always used to say to me, "Ken, don't do something good for somebody else just to get something back. Do it because it's the right thing to do—but you'll be amazed at how much good comes back to you."

When Susan talks about choice, connection, and competence, she wants you to flourish and to experience optimal motivation and well-being—not in a self-serving way but in a way where you can make a significant difference in the world. If you do it early, you'll be surprised by the "good" success that comes your direction.

Ken Blanchard, cofounder of The Ken Blanchard Companies and coauthor of more than sixty-five books, including *The New One Minute Manager* and *Leading at a Higher Level*.

NOTES

Introduction

1. Richard M. Ryan and Edward L. Deci, *Self-Determination Theory: Basic Psychological Needs in Motivation, Development, and Wellness* (New York: Guilford Press, 2017).
2. For more on the founding fathers of self-determination theory, see the bios for Edward L. Deci (http://www.sas.rochester.edu/psy /people/faculty/deci_edward/) and Richard M. Ryan (http://www.sas .rochester.edu/psy/people/faculty/ryan_richard/).

Chapter 1

1. My gratitude to Dr. Jacques Forest, professor and motivational psychologist for the School of Management Sciences at the University of Quebec at Montreal (ESG UQAM), for his contribution to this succinct overview of self-determination theory. Dr. Forest, Dr. Geneviève Mageau (professor at Université de Montréal), Dr. Joëlle Carpentier (professor at ESG UQAM), Jean-Paul Richard (former Olympic coach and now manager at Cirque du Soleil), and Sophie Gadoury (leadership program manager at Université de Montréal) are teaching people how to be more optimally functioning human beings through their collective company, reROOT. Visit www.reROOT inc.com for more information.

Chapter 2

1. Tom Rath and Jim Harter, *The Economics of Wellbeing* (Washington, DC: Gallup Consulting, 2010).
2. Hannele Huhtala and Marjo-Riitta Diehl, "A Review of Employee Well-Being and Innovativeness: An Opportunity for Mutual Benefit," *Creativity and Innovation Management* 16, no. 3 (2007): 299–306, https://doi.org/10.1111/j.14678691.2007.00442.x; and Peter Warr and Karina Nielsen, "Wellbeing and Work Performance," in *Handbook of Subjective Wellbeing*, eds. E. Diener, S. Oishi, and L. Tay (Salt Lake City, UT: DEF Publishers, 2018), https://www.nobascholar.com/chapters/69.
3. Karen Jeffrey et al. *Well-being at Work: A Review of the Literature* (London: New Economics Foundation, 2014), https://b.3cdn.net /nefoundation/71c1bb59a2ce151df7_8am6bqr2q.pdf.

4. Marylène Gagné, ed., *The Oxford Handbook of Work Engagement, Motivation, and Self-Determination Theory* (New York: Oxford University Press, 2014), 20–22.

Chapter 3

1. Viktor Frankl, *Man's Search for Meaning* (Boston: Beacon Press, 2006).
2. Frankl, 132.

Chapter 4

1. Ceylan Yeginsu, "U.K. Appoints a Minister for Loneliness," *New York Times*, January 17, 2018, https://www.nytimes.com/2018/01/17/world /europe/uk-britain-loneliness.html.
2. Julianne Holt-Lunstad, Timothy B. Smith, and J. Bradley Layton, "Social Relationships and Mortality Risk: A Meta-analytic Review," *PLoS Medicine* 7, no. 7 (2010): e1000316, https://doi.org/10.1371 /journal.pmed.1000316; C. Wilson and B. Moulton, Knowledge Networks and Insight Policy Research, *Loneliness among Older Adults: A National Survey of Adults 45+* (Washington, DC: AARP, 2010), https://assets.aarp.org/rgcenter/general/loneliness_2010.pdf; and Jane E. Brody, "Shaking Off Loneliness," *Well* (blog), *New York Times*, May 13, 2013, https://well.blogs.nytimes.com/2013/05/13 /shaking-off-loneliness.
3. Vivek Murthy, "Connecting at Work," *The Big Idea* (special report), HBR.org, September 2017, https://hbr.org/cover-story /2017/09/work-and-the-loneliness-epidemic; and Hakan Ozcelik and Sigal Barsade, "Work Loneliness and Employee Performance," *Academy of Management Proceedings* 2011, no. 1 (2011): 1–6, https://doi.org/10.5465/AMBPP.2011.65869714.

Chapter 5

1. Kirby L. J. Shannahan, Alan J. Bush, and Rachelle J. Shannahan, "Are Your Salespeople Coachable? How Salesperson Coachability, Trait Competitiveness, and Transformational Leadership Enhance Sales Performance," *Journal of the Academy of Marketing Science* 41, no. 1 (2013): 40–54, https://doi.org/10.1007/s11747-012-0302-9; and Michael P. Ciutcha et al., "Betting on the Coachable Entrepreneur: Signaling and Social Exchange in Entrepreneurial Pitches," *Entrepreneurship Theory and Practice* 42, no. 6 (2017): 860–885, https://doi .org/10.1177/1042258717725520.
2. Teresa Amabile and Steven Kramer, *The Progress Principle: Using Small Wins to Ignite Joy, Engagement, and Creativity at Work* (Boston: Harvard Business Review Press, 2011).
3. Marie Kondo, *The Life-Changing Magic of Tidying Up: The Japanese Art of Decluttering and Organizing* (Berkeley: Ten Speed Press, 2014).

Chapter 6

1. Edward Deci, email to author, August 8, 2016; and Edward L. Deci, Richard Koestner, and Richard M. Ryan, "A Meta-analytic Review of Experiments Examining the Effects of Extrinsic Rewards on Intrinsic Motivation," *Psychological Bulletin* 125, no. 6 (1999): 627–668, https://doi.org/10.1037/0033-2909.125.6.627.

2. Christopher P. Cerasoli, Jessica M. Nicklin, and Michael T. Ford, "Intrinsic Motivation and Extrinsic Incentives Jointly Predict Performance: A 40-Year Meta-analysis," *Psychological Bulletin* 140, no. 4 (2014): 980–1008, https://doi.org/10.1037/a0035661.

3. David Harrison, Meghna Virick, and Sonja William, "Working without a Net: Time, Performance, and Turnover under Maximally Contingent Rewards," *Journal of Applied Psychology* 81, no. 4 (1996): 331–345, https://doi.org/10.1037/0021-9010.81.4.331.

4. Deci, Koestner, and Ryan, "A Meta-analytic Review," 59.

5. David De Cremer, "Affective and Motivational Consequences of Leader Self-Sacrifice: The Moderating Effects of Autocratic Leadership," *Leadership Quarterly* 17, no. 1 (2006): 79–93, https://doi.org/10.1016/j.leaqua.2005.10.005; and Drea Zigarmi and Taylor P. Roberts, "Leader Values as Predictors of Employee Affect and Work Passion Intentions," *Journal of Modern Economy and Management* 1, no. 1 (2012): 1–32.

6. Miki Gandhi, translated by Mahadev Desai, *An Autobiography or The Story of My Experiments with Truth: A Critical Edition* (Yale University Press, 2018).

7. Edward L. Deci and Richard M. Ryan, "Facilitating Optimal Motivation and Psychological Well-Being Across Life Domains," *Canadian Psychology* 49, no. 1 (2008): 14–23.

Chapter 7

1. Self-regulation is defined as mindfully managing feelings, thoughts, values, and purpose for immediate and sustained positive effort. When you have low-quality self-regulation, you experience suboptimal motivation; high-quality self-regulation results in optimal motivation.

2. Drea Zigarmi et al., *The Leader within: Learning Enough about Yourself to Lead Others* (Upper Saddle River, NJ: FT Press, 2004).

3. Milton Rokeach, *Beliefs, Attitudes, and Values: A Theory of Organization and Change* (San Francisco: Jossey-Bass, 1968), 77.

4. Kirk Warren Brown and Richard M. Ryan, "The Benefits of Being Present: Mindfulness and Its Role in Psychological Well-Being," *Journal of Personality and Social Psychology* 84, no. 4 (2003): 822–848.

5. Abraham Maslow, *Motivation and Personality* (New York: Harper, 1954).
6. Edward L. Deci and Richard M. Ryan, "The Importance of Universal Psychological Needs for Understanding Motivation in the Workplace," in *The Oxford Handbook of Work Engagement, Motivation, and Self-Determination Theory*, ed. Marylène Gagné (New York: Oxford University Press, 2014), 13–32.

Chapter 8
1. Richard M. Ryan et al., "All Goals Are Not Created Equal Organismic Perspective on the Nature of Goals and Their Regulation," in *The Psychology of Action: Linking Cognition and Motivation to Behavior*, eds. P. M. Gollwitzer and John A. Bargh (New York, Guilford Press, 1996), 8.
2. Ellen Langer, "Mindfulness Isn't Much Harder Than Mindlessness," *Managing Yourself* (blog), HBR.org, January 13, 2016, https://hbr.org/2016/01/mindfulness-isnt-much-harder-than-mindlessness.
3. Jordan T. Quaglia et al., "Meta-analytic Evidence for Effects of Mindfulness Training on Dimensions of Self-Reported Dispositional Mindfulness," *Psychological Assessment* 28, no. 7 (2016), http://dx.doi.org/10.1037/pas0000268.
4. Arlen C. Moller et al., "Financial Motivation Undermines Maintenance in an Intensive Diet and Activity Intervention," *Journal of Obesity* 2012, no. 5 (2012): 1–8.

Part Three
1. Katie Mettler, "Rip Currents Swept Away a Florida Family. Then Beachgoers Formed a Human Chain," *Morning Mix* (blog), *Washington Post*, July 11, 2017, https://www.washingtonpost.com/news/morning-mix/wp/2017/07/11/a-riptide-swept-away-a-florida-family-then-beachgoers-formed-a-human-chain.
2. Jessica Mae Simmons, "So what is on my mind tonight?" Facebook, July 9, 2017, https://www.facebook.com/Jessiemae1691/posts/1539400839423658.

Chapter 9
1. Byron Katie, *Loving What Is: Four Questions That Can Change Your Life* (New York: Harmony Books, 2002).
2. The Work of Byron Katie, www.thework.com.

Chapter 10
1. Richard M. Ryan and Edward L. Deci, "Self-Determination Theory and the Facilitation of Intrinsic Motivation, Social Development, and Well-Being," *American Psychologist* 55, no. 1 (2000): 68.

2. Ryan and Deci, 68.
3. Tim Kasser, *The High Price of Materialism* (Chester, NJ: Bradford Book Company, 2003); and Kelly Kennedy, "Firms Bet Money Will Prod Employees to Health," *USA Today*, November 25, 2011.
4. Helga Dittmar, Rod Bond, Megan Hurst, and Tim Kasser, "The Relationship between Materialism and Personal Well-Being: A Meta-analysis," *Journal of Personality and Social Psychology* 107, no. 5 (2014): 879–924; and Tim Kasser et al., "Changes in Materialism, Changes in Psychological Well-Being: Evidence from Three Longitudinal Studies and an Intervention Experiment," *Motivation and Emotion* 38, no. 1 (2014): 1–22.
5. Kasser, *The High Price of Materialism*, 61–72.
6. Anias Thibault Landry et al., "Why Individuals Want Money Is What Matters: Using Self-Determination Theory to Explain the Differential Relationship between Motives for Making Money and Employee Psychological Health," *Motivation and Emotion* 40, no. 2 (2016), https://doi.org/10.1007/s11031-015-9532-8; Anias Thibault Landry, Ying Zhang, and Jacques Forest, "Applying Self-Determination Theory to Understand the Motivational Impact of Cash Rewards: New Evidence from Lab Experiments" (in submission, *European Journal of Social Psychology*, 2018); Anias Thibault et al., "Revisiting the Use of Cash Rewards in the Workplace: Evidence of Their Differential Impact on Employees' Experience in Three Studies Using Self-Determination Theory" (in submission, *Work and Occupations: An International Sociological Journal*, 2018); and Marylène Gagné and Jacques Forest, "The Study of Compensation Systems through the Lens of Self-Determination Theory: Reconciling 35 Years of Debate," *Canadian Psychology* 49, no. 3 (2008): 225–232.
7. Mark H. White and Kennon M. Sheldon, "The Contract Year Syndrome in the NBA and MLB: A Classic Undermining Pattern," *Motivation and Emotion* 38, no. 2 (2014): 196–205.
8. Joseph E. Stiglitz, *The Price of Inequality: How Today's Divided Society Endangers Our Future* (New York: W. W. Norton, 2012): 146–186.
9. Daniel Kahneman and Angus Deaton, "High Income Improves Evaluation of Life but Not Emotional Well-Being," *Proceedings of the National Academy of Sciences* 107, no. 38 (2010): 16489–16493, doi:10.1073/pnas.1011492107.
10. Matthew D. Lieberman, *Social: Why Our Brains Are Wired to Connect* (New York: Broadway Books, 2013).
11. Online Etymology Dictionary, s.v., "happy," accessed October 17, 2018, https://www.etymonline.com/classic/search?q=happy.

12. Robert J. Vallerand et al., "Les Passions de l'Âme: On Obsessive and Harmonious Passion," *Journal of Personality and Social Psychology* 85, no. 4 (2003): 756–767.

Chapter 11

1. Susan Fowler et al., "A Business Case for Optimal Motivation" (white paper), The Ken Blanchard Companies, 2016, https://resources.www.kenblanchard.comwhitepapers/a-business-case-for-optimal-motivation.
2. Heidi Grant, "The Neuroscience of Better Feedback" (webinar), NeuroLeadership Institute, July 19, 2017, https://neuroleadership.com/portfolio-items/improve-feedback-july2017/.
3. Grant, "Neuroscience."
4. Grant, "Neuroscience."
5. Pascal-Emmanuel Gobry, "The Real Reason Wells Fargo Employees Resorted to Fraud," *The Week*, October 3, 2016, http://theweek.com/articles/652186/real-reason-wells-fargo-employees-resorted-fraud.
6. Kevin Wack, "Wells Fargo's Latest Troubles Suggest Tougher Stance by OCC," Bankshot (blog), *American Banker*, December 6, 2018, https://www.americanbanker.com/opinion/wells-fargos-latest-troubles-suggest-tougher-stance-by-OCC.
7. Alexandre J. S. Morin et al., "Longitudinal Associations between Employees' Beliefs about the Quality of the Change Management Process, Affective Commitment to Change and Psychological Empowerment," *Human Relations* 69, no. 3 (2016): 839–867; Drea Zigarmi, Susan Fowler, and Dobie Houson, "Developing Self Leaders—A Competitive Advantage for Organizations" (white paper), The Ken Blanchard Companies, 2017, https://resources.kenblanchard.com/whitepapers/developing-self-leaders and Chia-huei Wu and Sharon Parker, "Thinking and Acting in Anticipation: A Review of Research on Proactive Behavior,"*Advances in Psychological Science* 21, no. 4 (2012): 679–700.

Chapter 12

1. Kenneth H. Blanchard et al., *Leading at a Higher Level: Blanchard on Leadership and Creating High Performing Organizations*, 3rd ed. (Upper Saddle River, NJ: Financial Times Press, 2018); Pat Zigarmi and Judd Hockstra, Leading People through Change Workshop, The Ken Blanchard Companies.

RESOURCES

Master Your Motivation Bonus Material
Visit *Master Your Motivation* on Susan's website for bonus material and video clips related to each chapter. You will also find a free survey to help you identify your motivational outlook, links for webinars and podcasts, blog posts, and additional resources at www.susanfowler.com.

CHOMP Newsletter
If you are optimally motivated to continue learning, practicing, and applying the skill of motivation, sign up for Susan's monthly *CHOMP Newsletter* at http://www.susanfowler.com.

Keynotes and Consulting
To inquire about booking Susan for keynotes, consulting, or virtual book club events, email her at susan@susanfowler.com.

Training and Workshops
To inquire about workshops codeveloped by Susan on motivation and self leadership, contact The Ken Blanchard Companies at +1-760-489-5005 and Inspire Software at www.inspiresoftware.com.

More Books by Susan Fowler
You can find Susan's books online and in bookstores, including *Why Motivating People Doesn't Work . . . and What Does*, and *Self Leadership and The One Minute Manager,* coauthored with Ken Blanchard.

You can also find blogs and podcasts featuring Susan at www.LeaderChat.org and www.SmartBrief.com.

ACKNOWLEDGMENTS

E xpressing gratitude is a source of joy. It's also painful because I don't have enough pages to recognize everyone who has helped evolve the ideas in this book—or been a positive influence on me personally. If you don't find your name listed, please trust how much I appreciate you—from work associates and clients, workshop participants, keynote audiences, and *CHOMP Newsletter* readers to social media friends and connections. You have all played a key role in creating the choice, connection, and competence needed to take the complex science of motivation to the other side of complexity.

My Ken Blanchard Companies Family
Profound gratitude to Ken and Margie Blanchard and the KBC founding associates, leadership team, and associates for the opportunity to participate in their mission of unleashing the potential and power in people and organizations for the greater good. Special thanks to

Business developers who advocate for optimal motivation with their clients, especially Trey S., John H., Michelle S., Wendy V., Stacy A., Ken W., Darren Y., Jackie G., Patrick M., Mark F., and Mark M.

Consulting partners who teach optimal motivation and are masters of motivation, especially Judith D., Els K., Rares M., Phil R., Calla C., Nancy B., John H., John L., Mark P., Peter B., Damon L., Lael G., MJ C., Ann P., and Maria P.

Richard P. and Paul M., who coordinate and promote my work around the world with Blanchard Global Partners, including Stephanie M. and Mike L. in Korea, Anna K. and her team in Russia, Hisham E. and his team in Egypt, Spiros P. and his team in Greece, Marija P. in Serbia, Viorel P. in Romania, Jacinta R. in Singapore, Erez A. in Israel, Tao and his team throughout China, Ian B. and Andrew M. down under, and Malcolm S. and David C. in New Zealand.

Product development, especially Jay C., Gary O., Victoria C., Kelie S., Kim K., and Vanessa G.

Renee B., for her editing expertise.

Custom development, especially Erin J. and Melanie D.

The marketing department, especially David W., Vicki S., Stefanie H., Debbie B., Lisa P., Vanessa L., Monique S., and special acknowledgment to Patrick P. for his contribution to the cover design.

In Their Own Words

Dozens of people sent me their stories about mastering their motivation. I was humbled and grateful to include many of them in this book. I hope you continue practicing the skill of motivation and send me updates for future books!

CHOMP (Community of Healthy Optimal Motivational Pioneers)

Thanks go to

The Inspire Software and Innova Systems staff members, who were instrumental in the evolution of simplifying the skill of motivation, especially Chris W., Lynn H., Jason A., Ashley A., Chad C., Mike M., James K., Tom T, and Adam S.

Values-based clients, especially Tom H., Julia A., Nermine Z., and Nadia S.

Students, administrators, and faculty in the University of San Diego's Master of Science in Executive Leadership program—a robust learning lab over the past twenty years.

Respected colleagues and friends, Taylor P., Eileen H., Dick T., Amy P., Deb K., Billy Y., Carey N., Mattias B., Mattias D., and the Dahlgren clan.

The self-determination theory research community, especially Edward Deci, Richard Ryan, Jacques Forest, Marylène Gagné, Kennon Sheldon, Kirk Warren-Brown, Scott Rigby, and Shannon Hoefen.

My "kids," who are represented literally, figuratively, and lovingly throughout this book—Blair, Andrew, and Ferris F.; Alexa, Ryan, Evey, and Maggie T.; and Lisa Z. and Paul D. Special shout-out to Grant C. for his input on the cover design!

My PR super-duper team at Weaving Influence, who help spread these ideas around the world, especially Becky R., Kristin E., Whitney H., Aubrey K., Janeile M., Christy K., and Amy D.

Codevelopers of the Spectrum of Motivation model, Dr. Drea Zigarmi and Dr. David Facer.

The Berrett-Koehler Publishers Community
I wish I could name the entire staff, who generate the most positive working environment I've experienced. Alas, space is limited, so please know I appreciate all of you, especially my editor, Neal M.; my shepherd, Jeevan S.; and the man behind BK's values, Steve P. The sales and marketing team, especially Kristen F., Michael C., Katie S., Leslie C., Zoe M., Shabnam M., and Matt F. The production team, especially Edward W., Lasell W., Courtney S., and Chloe W. The foreign rights team, especially María Jesús A. and Catherine L. PeopleSpeak, editors extraordinaire, especially Sharon Goldinger for making me a better writer. And the reviewers who provided constructive and inspiring feedback, Valerie A., Buddy B., Candace S., and Ken F.

INDEX

Page references followed by *fig* indicate an illustrated figure.

actions, 136–138, 144, 147, 151–154. *See also* choice, connection, and competence actions
Adam's story, 95–97
advocating for justice, 146–149
agentic tendency, 127
airport security story, 152–154
aliens in Mall of America story, 47
aligned motivational outlook, 49*fig*–50, 59–63, 69–70
aneurysm story, 79–81
Anya's story, 51
"Art of Persuasion, The" program, 107
authentic life, 135–138

bad habit story, 70–71
Barry's story, 56–57
beliefs, 74–75, 158. *See also* credo ("I believe")
belonging, 33, 36
blaming others, 25, 27
blaming Sam story, 76–78
Blanchard, Ken, 98, 159–162
blouse story, 54–55
Brenda's story, 85–87
Brett's story, 38–39
Buford, Bob, 161
busyness fatal distraction, 135–138

Calla's story, 104–105
change, 150, 151–158
choice
  concerns, questions, and ways to create, 24–29, 60–71, 75–76, 155
  stories on making, 70–77, 79–81
choice, connection, and competence actions
  eroding, 19*fig*, 20
  stories on, 11–14, 82–90, 98–104

strategies for creating, 8–10, 15–16, 19*fig*, 22, 68–70, 81–82, 142
three scientific truths on, 8–9
  See also actions
collaborative spontaneous moments, 109–111
competence, 37–42, 69–71, 156
connection, 30–36, 69–71, 145–146, 156
credo ("I believe"), 80–85. *See also* beliefs

death and renewal cycle, 157–158
Deborah's story, 72–73
Deci, Edward, 2, 58, 66, 127
developed values, 61–63, 72, 74
dieting motivation, 98–102, 120–124
discipline as red flag, 22
disconnecting from busyness, 135–138
disinterested motivational outlook, 49*fig*, 52–53, 69–70
Dobie's story, 37–38
Drea (author's husband), 92, 98–102

Eileen's story, 106–108
espoused values, 71–72
external motivational outlook, 49*fig*–50, 53–55, 69–70, 161–162. *See also* rewards/incentives
extrinsic motivation, 2, 3, 19

fatal distractions, 126–138, 161. *See also* work hazards
fears, 115
feedback, 39, 142–146, 148–149
feelings and mindfulness, 92–97
flipping the feedback, 142–146, 160
Forest, Jacques, 134
Frankl, Viktor, 25–26
freedom vs. choice, 25–26

Gandhi, 25, 62–63

Gina's story, 116–117
goals
  creating choice, connection, and
  competence to achieve, 22, 39,
  75–76, 104–105, 146
  motivation to pursue, 2, 3, 9,
  65–67
  Wells Fargo Bank scandal due to
  unrealistic, 147
gratitude, 80, 152–154

Halftime (Buford), 161
Hamlet (Shakespeare), 125
happiness, 128–135, 161
Heckler, Lou, 66
"How to Write a Business Plan"
  seminar, 107

*I Am Malala: The Girl Who Stood Up
  for Education and Was Shot by the
  Taliban* (Yousafzai), 10
identifying your outlook
  author on mastering her own
  motivation by, 151
  introduction to, 47–48*fig*, 89*fig*
  Master Your Motivation web page
  on, 67
  as motivation skill action, 44*fig*
  three optimal motivational outlooks, 49*fig*, 50–51, 59–67
  three suboptimal motivational outlooks, 49*fig*–50, 51–57
  what science says about, 58
imposed motivational outlook,
  49*fig*–50, 55–57, 69–70, 113–114
"in the zone," 65
incentives. *See* rewards/incentives
inherent motivational outlook,
  49*fig*–51, 65–67, 69–70
Instagram, 30
integrated motivational outlook,
  49*fig*–51, 63–65, 69–70
intrinsic motivation, 2, 3, 19, 65–67
Ivan's story, 82–85

Josie's story, 88–90
journaling, 123

"Judge-Your-Neighbor Worksheet,
  The," 118
judgments, 117–120
Judith's story, 76–78
junk food motivation, 15, 21–23,
  116–117
justice advocation, 146–149

Katie, Byron, 117–120
Ken Blanchard Companies, The, 162
King, Martin Luther, Jr., 25
know yourself, 125–126
Kondo, Marie, 41
kung fu story, 93–94

Langer, Ellen, 91
Leading at a Higher Level
  (Blanchard), 162
Lee's story, 64–65
listening, 136–137, 142–146, 160
loneliness, 34–35
Louise's story, 113, 115

Major League Baseball players, 130
Mandela, Nelson, 25
Man's Search for Meaning (Frankl),
  25–26
Mark's story, 102–104
Marty's story, 113, 114–115
Maslow, Abraham, 2, 79
Master Your Motivation web page
  on change, 158
  on creating choice, 29
  on creating competence, 45
  on fatal distractions, 138
  on identifying your motivational
  outlook, 67
  on reflecting on your outlook,
  111
  on shifting your motivational outlook, 87, 125
mastering motivation stories, 132,
  135, 151–154
materialism, 128–132, 161
#MeToo movement, 25
mindfulness, 91–108, 123, 158
mindlessness, 91–92

minister for loneliness (UK, 2018),
34–35
Missy's story, 145–146
Mitchell, Stephen, 118
motivation
extrinsic, 2, 3, 19
intrinsic, 2, 3, 19, 65–67
junk food, 15, 21–23, 116–117
stories on mastering, 132–135,
151–154
understanding the nature of, 1,
17–21, 43–45
motivation science
on fatal distractions, 127
on identifying your motivational
outlook, 58
on mindfulness, 97
on motivational outlooks, 44fig,
47–49
on optimal motivation, 20
on pursuit of material wealth,
129–130
on self-determination theory,
14–16
on the Spectrum of Motivation
model, 18–19fig, 69–70
three scientific truths of, 5–36
motivation skills
"identify your outlook" action to
build, 44fig, 47–67, 48fig, 151
Judith's story on applying,
76–78
"reflect on your outlook" action to
build, 44fig, 47–48fig, 88–108,
153–154
"shift your outlook" action to
build, 44fig, 47–48fig, 68–87,
151–153
motivation theories
number of discredited, 1–2
self-determination theory (SDT),
2, 14–16
Spectrum of Motivation model,
49fig, 69–70
motivational outlooks
identifying your, 44fig, 47–67,
48fig, 89fig, 151

reflect on your, 44fig, 47–48fig,
68–87, 88–108, 109–111,
153–154
shift your, 44fig, 47–48fig, 88–108,
89fig, 151–153

National Basketball Association
players, 130
New One Minute Manager, The
(Blanchard), 162
Nick's story, 21–22

obsessive passion, 135–136
One Minute Praisings, 159–160
optimal motivation, 19fig–20
optimal motivational outlooks
aligned, 49fig, 50, 59, 60–63
inherent, 49fig, 51, 59–60, 65–67
integrated, 49fig, 50–51, 59, 63–65
looking deeper into, 59–60
stories on, 98–102, 106–108,
120–123
outlooks. See motivational outlooks

Panama City Beach human chain
story, 110–111
Patricia's story, 120–123
Phil's life credo story, 79–81
physical sensations, 94
Polonius (Hamlet character), 125
Potato Chip Rock photo op (Poway,
CA), 31–33
psychological junk food, 15
"psychological vitamins," 15–16
purpose, 64–65, 80, 137

reshifting stories, 98–102, 106–108,
120–123
reflecting on your outlook
author's mastering her own motivation using, 153–154
introduction to, 44fig, 47–48fig,
89fig
Master Your Motivation web page
on, 111
mindfulness for, 90–92, 98–106
stories on, 88–90, 102–111

reflecting on your outlook, (*continued*)
reframing a task story, 104–105
reticular activation, 9–10
rewards/incentives, 49*fig*–50, 53–55, 58, 139–142, 161–162. *See also* external motivational outlook
Rocio's story, 148–149
Roland's story, 70–71
Ryan, Richard, 2, 127

Science Says. *See* motivation science
Second Secret of the One Minute Manager–One Minute Praisings, 159–160
self-actualization, 78–79
self-awareness, 74–75, 124–125
self-determination theory (SDT), 2, 14–16
shifting barriers, 113–125
shifting your outlook
    introduction and strategies on, 44*fig*, 47–48*fig*, 68–75, 78–85, 89*fig*
    Master Your Motivation web page on, 87, 125
    stories on, 76–87, 151–153
Simmons, Derek, 110
Simmons, Jessica, 110–111
singer's audition story, 39
Skinner, B. F., 2
smoking stories, 70–71, 115
social media, 30–31
Spectrum of Motivation model, 49*fig*, 69–70
Spiros's story, 124–125
Stacy-Diane story, 11–14
"state of flow," 65
suboptimal motivation, 19*fig*, 20–22, 127
suboptimal motivational outlooks
    disinterested, 49*fig*, 52–53
    external, 49*fig*–50, 53–55
    imposed, 49*fig*, 50, 55–57, 113–114

rewards as a work hazard and form of, 139–142
swimmers' human chain rescue story, 110–111

thriving, 8–9, 14–15
tree limb story, 109, 111

unplanned moments, 67

value statements, 71–72
values
    aligned motivational outlook based on, 59
    aligning actions and choices with, 70–76, 124, 147
    all beliefs are, 75
    developed, 61–62, 72, 74
    espoused, 71–72
    materialistic, 128–132, 161
    programmed, 61
    stories on, 56–57, 72–73
    understanding the source of your, 74–75
    used to break through fears, 115
vegetarianism, 43–44, 62–64
video gaming addiction, 33–34

Wells Fargo Bank scandal, 147
"What Do You Value?" exercise, 71–74
Why Motivating People Doesn't Work . . . and What Does (Fowler), 4
willpower red flag, 22
work hazards, 49*fig*–50, 53–55, 58, 139–143. *See also* fatal distractions
"Work, The" process of inquiry, 117–120
workplace, 142–149, 160
World Health Organization, 33

Yousafzai, Malala, 10, 25

ABOUT THE AUTHOR

Ryan Talbot

In her bestselling book, *Why Motivating People Doesn't Work . . . and What Does*, Susan implored leaders to stop trying to motivate people because it just doesn't work and aggravates everyone involved. She provided best practices for increasing productivity and work passion through a tested framework and process for helping people shift the quality of their motivation. Thousands of managers worldwide have learned how to activate their staff members' optimal motivation. Now Susan is on a mission to help individuals master their own motivation, achieve their goals, and flourish as they succeed.

Widely known as one of the foremost experts on motivation and personal empowerment, Susan gained her knowledge through extensive experience in business, advertising, sales, production, marketing, executive and lifestyle coaching, and leadership training in all fifty states and forty foreign countries with clients as diverse as AARP, AkzoNobel, Alix Partners, Apple, Bayer Healthcare, Chamberlain Group, Dow, Eli Lilly, Fruit of the Loom, Google, Harley-Davidson, Kawasaki, McGill University Health Center, Mattel, the National Basketball Association, and Xerox.

Susan is the coauthor of the innovative Optimal Motivation product line for The Ken Blanchard Companies as well as the creator and lead developer of Self Leadership, its best-in-class self leadership and personal empowerment program.

She was given the Lifetime Achievement Award for instructional design from the North American Simulations and Gaming Association.

Susan has published in peer-reviewed academic journals and is the coauthor of three books with Ken Blanchard: *Self Leadership and The One Minute Manager®*, *Leading at a Higher Level: Blanchard on Leadership and Creating High Performing Organizations*, and *Empowerment*. She coauthored *Achieve Leadership Genius: How You Lead Depends on Who, What, Where, and When You Lead* with Drea Zigarmi and Dick Lyles.

Susan lives with her husband, Drea Zigarmi, in San Diego where she is a senior consulting partner for The Ken Blanchard Companies, a leadership consultant and motivation coach, and a professor in the Master of Science in Executive Leadership program at the University of San Diego. Susan is a rotating board member for Angel Faces, a nonprofit organization serving adolescent girls with severe burn trauma and disfigurements.

www.susanfowler.com

More from Susan Fowler

Why Motivating People Doesn't Work...and What Does

The New Science of Leading, Energizing, and Engaging

Stop Trying to Motivate People!

In her bestselling book, top leadership researcher, consultant, and speaker Susan Fowler reveals best practices for increasing productivity and work passion. Her Optimal Motivation approach provides leaders with a field-tested framework and process for helping people discover how their jobs can satisfy the psychological needs—for autonomy, relatedness, and competence—that lead to meaningful and sustainable motivation. Illustrated throughout with real-life examples, Fowler's book is the groundbreaking answer for leaders who want to get motivation right!

Hardcover, 232 pages, ISBN 978-1-62656-182-3
Paperback, 232 pages, ISBN 978-1-62656-945-4
PDF ebook, ISBN 978-1-62656-183-0
ePub ebook ISBN 978-1-62656-184-7

Berrett–Koehler Publishers, Inc.
www.bkconnection.com   **800.929.2929**

Berrett–Koehler
Publishers

Berrett-Koehler is an independent publisher dedicated to an ambitious mission: *Connecting people and ideas to create a world that works for all.*

Our publications span many formats, including print, digital, audio, and video. We also offer online resources, training, and gatherings. And we will continue expanding our products and services to advance our mission.

We believe that the solutions to the world's problems will come from all of us, working at all levels: in our society, in our organizations, and in our own lives. Our publications and resources offer pathways to creating a more just, equitable, and sustainable society. They help people make their organizations more humane, democratic, diverse, and effective (and we don't think there's any contradiction there). And they guide people in creating positive change in their own lives and aligning their personal practices with their aspirations for a better world.

And we strive to practice what we preach through what we call "The BK Way." At the core of this approach is *stewardship,* a deep sense of responsibility to administer the company for the benefit of all of our stakeholder groups, including authors, customers, employees, investors, service providers, sales partners, and the communities and environment around us. Everything we do is built around stewardship and our other core values of *quality, partnership, inclusion,* and *sustainability.*

This is why Berrett-Koehler is the first book publishing company to be both a B Corporation (a rigorous certification) and a benefit corporation (a for-profit legal status), which together require us to adhere to the highest standards for corporate, social, and environmental performance. And it is why we have instituted many pioneering practices (which you can learn about at www.bkconnection.com), including the Berrett-Koehler Constitution, the Bill of Rights and Responsibilities for BK Authors, and our unique Author Days.

We are grateful to our readers, authors, and other friends who are supporting our mission. We ask you to share with us examples of how BK publications and resources are making a difference in your lives, organizations, and communities at www.bkconnection.com/impact.

Dear reader,

Thank you for picking up this book and welcome to the worldwide BK community! You're joining a special group of people who have come together to create positive change in their lives, organizations, and communities.

What's BK all about?

Our mission is to connect people and ideas to create a world that works for all.

Why? Our communities, organizations, and lives get bogged down by old paradigms of self-interest, exclusion, hierarchy, and privilege. But we believe that can change. That's why we seek the leading experts on these challenges—and share their actionable ideas with you.

A welcome gift

To help you get started, we'd like to offer you a **free copy** of one of our bestselling ebooks:

www.bkconnection.com/welcome

When you claim your **free ebook**, you'll also be subscribed to our blog.

Our freshest insights

Access the best new tools and ideas for leaders at all levels on our blog at ideas.bkconnection.com.

Sincerely,

Your friends at Berrett-Koehler

MIX
Paper from
responsible sources
FSC® C008955

Certified

Corporation